Presbyterians Being Reformed

*Reflections on What
the Church Needs Today*

Edited by

Robert H. Bullock Jr.

Geneva Press
Louisville, Kentucky

Book design by Sharon Adams
Cover design by Pam Poll Graphic Design

First edition
Published by Geneva Press
Louisville, Kentucky

This book is printed on acid-free paper that meets the American National Standards Institute Z39.48 standard. ♾

PRINTED IN THE UNITED STATES OF AMERICA

06 07 08 09 10 11 12 13 14 15—10 9 8 7 6 5 4 3 2 1

Library of Congress Cataloging-in-Publication Data

Presbyterians being reformed : reflections on what the church needs today / Robert H.
    Bullock, Jr., editor.
        p. cm.
    Includes bibliographical references.
    ISBN-13: 978-0-664-50279-9 alk. paper
    ISBN-10: 0-664-50279-2
    1. Presbyterian Church (U.S.A.)   2. Church renewal.   3. Church.   4. Christianity—
Forecasting.   5. Twenty-first century—Forecasts.   I. Bullock, Robert H.

BX8969.2.P74   2006
285'.137—dc22   2005052657

Contents

Contributors

The Rev. Dr. Robert H. Bullock Jr. is resource developer for the United Way of Selma and Dallas County, Alabama; religion writer for *The Selma Times-Journal*; and a freelance writer and consultant. He is retired editor of *The Presbyterian Outlook*, a national independent weekly serving the PC(USA), where he worked for fifteen years. Previous church service included positions in new church development in Allen, Texas; in pastorates in Lynchburg, Virginia, and Austin, Texas; and as director of an ecumenical ministry in Fulton, Missouri. He has published several scholarly articles and contributed a chapter to the seven-volume Lilly Foundation series on the PC(USA).

The Rev. Dr. Clifton Kirkpatrick is stated clerk (chief ecclesiastical officer) of the Presbyterian Church (U.S.A.). He is also the president of the World Alliance of Reformed Churches. He served previously as director of the Worldwide Ministries Division, where he led the Presbyterian Church's ministries in the United States and more than eighty other nations in the areas of evangelism, education, health, world service, and development. He also serves on the governing board of the National Council of Churches of Christ in the U.S.A., the World Council of Churches, and the Council of Presidents, United States Chapter of the World Conference on Religion and Peace.

The Rev. Dr. Anna Case-Winters is professor of theology at McCormick Theological Seminary. Following her theological studies, she served a pastorate in Oklahoma City and as associate director of field education and graduate teaching scholar at Vanderbilt University, where she completed her doctoral studies. She has served on the Caribbean and North American Area Council of the World Alliance of Reformed Churches and on the General Assembly Committee on Ecumenical Relations. She has been named cochair of the new Lutheran-Reformed Joint International Commission. She has written one book: *Divine Power: Traditional Understandings and Contemporary*

Challenges. She is currently working on a second book tentatively titled, *Down to Earth: A Christian Theology of Nature.*

The Rev. Dr. Fahed Abu-Akel is founder and executive director of Atlanta Ministry with International Students, Inc., and national director of the Christmas International House program in fifty cities. Both ministries are located at Peachtree Presbyterian Church, Atlanta. He has served as an adjunct faculty member at Interdenominational Theological Center. He served on the mission staff of First Presbyterian Church, Atlanta. He served as moderator of the 214th General Assembly of the PC(USA) (2002–2003). He has served on the boards of many national and local organizations and has received a number of awards and recognitions for service. He continues to speak on the mission of the church around the country.

Scott D. Anderson is executive director of the Wisconsin Council of Churches. A former Presbyterian minister, he served for twelve years on the staff of the California Council of Churches, the last six as executive director, prior to his election to his current position in March 2003. While in California, he organized four important public education initiatives for the California religious community involving health and welfare reform, violence prevention among California youth, and the growth of religious pluralism. He served California pastorates in North Highlands and in Sacramento. Anderson has broad ecumenical experience and has received awards for distinguished service in both the public and private sectors.

The Rev. Dr. Jerry Andrews is pastor of First Presbyterian Church, Glen Ellyn, Illinois, and serves as moderator of the Presbyterian Coalition, an advocacy group within the PC(USA). After graduation from seminary he served a pastorate in Hookstown, Pennsylvania, followed by interim pastorates at Presbyterian churches in Lombard and Downers Grove, Pennsylvania. His pastorate in Glen Ellyn began in 1992. He is active in the life of Chicago Presbytery and denominational affairs. Long-term special interests include classical, biblical, and historical studies.

The Rev. Dr. Susan Andrews has served as pastor of Bradley Hills Presbyterian Church, Bethesda, Maryland, since 1989. Previous service included pastorates in East Hanover, New Jersey; Allentown, Pennsylvania; and as acting chaplain at her alma mater, Wellesley College. She served as moderator of the 215th General Assembly of the PC(USA) (2003–2004). Other church service includes membership on the General Assembly Council, as moderator of National Capital and Newton presbyteries, and as chair of the General

Assembly Call System Task Force. She has contributed sermons to lectionary resource publications and has received awards for her preaching.

The Rev. Dr. John Buchanan has served as pastor of Fourth Presbyterian Church, Chicago, since 1985 and is editor/publisher of *The Christian Century*. He served as moderator of the 208th General Assembly of the PC(USA) (1996–97). Other pastorates served include churches in Columbus, Ohio, and Lafayette and Dyer, Indiana. He has also served as presbytery moderator, as a member of the governing board of the National Council of Churches of Christ in the U.S.A., and as an observer to the Seventh Assembly of the World Council of Churches in Canberra, Australia. He is president of the Board of Trustees of McCormick Theological Seminary. Buchanan has received several honorary doctorates and is author of *Being Church, Becoming Community* and, with Elam Davies, *Sermons for the City.*

The Rev. Dr. Jack Haberer is editor-in-chief of *The Presbyterian Outlook* based in Richmond, Virginia. He most recently served as pastor of Clear Lake Presbyterian Church in Houston from 1994 to 2005. He previously served pastorates in Satellite Beach and Pompano Beach, Florida. He served three years as moderator of the Presbyterian Coalition, an independent advocacy group in the PC(USA), and six years on the board of Presbyterians for Renewal, also an independent advocacy group, including one year as president. He also served on the General Assembly planning committee for the Conference on Unity and Diversity and then on the Theological Task Force on Peace, Unity, and Purity of the Church. He is author of *GodViews: The Convictions that Drive Us and Divide Us* and *Living the Presence of the Spirit.*

The Rev. Dr. William Stacy Johnson is the Arthur M. Adams Associate Professor of Theology at Princeton Theological Seminary. He previously served on the faculty at Austin Presbyterian Theological Seminary and was theologian-in-residence for four years at Westlake Hills Presbyterian Church in Austin. In addition to being an ordained Presbyterian minister, he is an attorney at law. He is the author of numerous books and articles, including *The Mystery of God: Karl Barth and the Postmodern Foundations of Theology.* He serves on the Theological Task Force on Peace, Unity, and Purity of the Church. He is also codirector of a Jewish-Christian-Muslim scriptural reasoning group at the Center of Theological Inquiry in Princeton.

The Rev. Dr. Curtis A. Jones is managing partner of CURESolutions, a Georgia-based consulting company specializing in church and community development. He was formerly the executive director of the National Black

Presbyterian Caucus. Prior to entering the ministry he was an organizer and negotiator for the National Hospital Workers Union in New Jersey, the American Federation of State, County, and Municipal Employees. He has served pastorates in Dallas and Baltimore. He has served on numerous community boards and denominational committees, including a special General Assembly task force on procurement and employment polices and practices relative to persons of color among the agencies of the PC(USA).

The Rev. Dr. Richard Ray serves as general editor of the Kerygma Program and as director of the Children's Trust Society of the Grandfather Home for Children in North Carolina. He spent twenty years in the pastorate, the last parish being First Presbyterian Church, Bristol, Tennessee. In addition, he has taught at Stephens College, King College, and Pittsburgh Theological Seminary. For nine years he was managing director of John Knox Press in the former Presbyterian Church U.S.

The Rev. Dr. Laird J. Stuart has been pastor of Calvary Presbyterian Church, San Francisco, since 1993. He has served pastorates in Grand Haven, Michigan; Bergenfield, New Jersey; and Milford, Connecticut. He is a member of the Board of Trustees of San Francisco Theological Seminary and recently served as president of the San Francisco Interfaith Council. He has received honorary doctorates from two insitutions.

The Rev. Michael R. Walker is the executive director of Presbyterians for Renewal, an independent advocacy group in the PC(USA), and a PhD candidate in history of doctrine at Princeton Theological Seminary. His dissertation topic is "John Calvin's Earliest Theology," exploring the Reformer's understanding of the immortality of the soul and its implications for the Christian life. He and his family live in Louisville, Kentucky, where Presbyterians for Renewal is based. Walker is the youngest of the contributors and therefore represents a significant group—ministers under the age of 40—in the life of the PC(USA).

Barbara G. Wheeler has been president of Auburn Seminary for twenty-two years. She also serves as director of Auburn's Center for the Study of Theological Education, founded in 1991. She consults widely with seminaries, denominations, and congregations concerned about the future of religious leadership and religious institutions. She is a member of the PC(USA); an elder in Peniel Presbyterian Church in Granville, New York; a member of the board of the Covenant Network of Presbyterians, an independent advocacy group in the PC(USA); and a member of the Theological Task Force on Peace, Unity, and Purity of the Church.

The Rev. Dr. Parker T. Williamson is chief executive officer of the Presbyterian Lay Committee, Inc., where he has served since 1988. He previously served pastorates in Lenoir, North Carolina; Lutz, Florida; and New Orleans. He has served as president of Caldwell County Hospice and on the boards of a number of local organizations and denominational bodies. He has traveled extensively on several continents as a journalist, preacher, and lecturer. He has served as chair of the Presbyterian Renewal Leaders Network; as vice chair of the Association for Church Renewal; and as a member of the boards of Reformed Fellowship International, Knox Fellowship, Literacy and Evangelism International, and the Howard Center. He has received two honorary doctorates.

Editor's Preface

*T*his volume, containing a spectrum of views of Presbyterian leaders on the current state of the Presbyterian Church (U.S.A.) and its prospects in the first decade of the twenty-first century, is intended for Presbyterian adults.

It is designed to be used in adult church school classes, especially those that use quarterly materials, and in other educational settings in the PC(USA) as well as for individual study.

Background material for the study is contained in an introductory section titled "Orienting Perspectives." Included are essays by the editor, PC(USA) stated clerk Clifton Kirkpatrick, and Professor Anna Case-Winters of McCormick Theological Seminary. The editor provides background material of a historical nature, the stated clerk comments on the nature and mission of the Presbyterian Church (U.S.A.), and Professor Case-Winters explains the meaning of the Presbyterian motto "Reformed and Always to Be Reformed."

Then follow the thirteen chapters containing the spectrum of perspectives on the theme "What the Presbyterian Church (U.S.A.) Needs Today." Every attempt has been made to achieve balance and inclusiveness in terms of views. At the end of each chapter are questions for discussion.

Church school teachers may devise their own methods of using the book, but if the adult class is on a quarterly basis, the whole class can read the introductory section at the beginning and discuss one chapter each week.

Unless otherwise indicated, all Scripture quotations are from the New Revised Standard Version of the Bible.

While this volume was designed for church school classes, because of the nature of the material and those contributing, it should enjoy wider use throughout the church at this time when there is considerable division in the church at large over sexuality and related issues.

On behalf of all the contributors, we hope that this resource serves the church well and will facilitate the kind of conversation that we must have if we are to hold together as a denomination in these difficult times.

Orienting Perspectives

Toward a New Presbyterian Church for a New Century

Robert H. Bullock Jr.

*I*t has been more than two decades since the formation of the Presbyterian Church (U.S.A.). That event came after more than a third of a century of sustained effort that occasioned almost continuous controversy over issues such as biblical authority and interpretation, theology, race, the role of women, and union itself.

The Presbyterian Church (U.S.A.) was formed in 1983 with the union of the United Presbyterian Church in the United States of America and the Presbyterian Church in the United States.

The two streams—the so-called northern and southern—were themselves the product of a division that occurred in 1861 as a direct consequence of the Civil War. In fact, in 1861, before the break, there were two Presbyterian General Assemblies, crossing sectional lines, resulting from an earlier division in 1838.

The United Presbyterian Church U.S.A. was the product of the reunion of the northern Old and New School General Assemblies in 1869, later joined by part of the Cumberland Presbyterian Church in 1906, the Welsh Calvinistic Methodist Church in 1920, and the United Presbyterian Church of North America in 1958. The Presbyterian Church U.S. was founded as the Presbyterian Church in the Confederate States of America in 1861 and, with some additions at the end of the Civil War, remained essentially the same ecclesiastical body until 1983.

Given the degree of conflict within the two uniting churches prior to the 1983 reunion, it was not surprising that there would be major conflicts in the new denomination in the years following.

A Century of Conflict within the Presbyterian Church

For nearly a hundred years there had been a growing polarity between liberals and conservatives in the Presbyterian Church. It reached its peak in the 1920s in the fundamentalist-modernist controversy in the then-Presbyterian

Church U.S.A. Similar tensions wracked the Presbyterian Church U.S., but always later and always to a lesser degree.

Following the 1983 reunion, there was a reaching out from like-minded groups in the two former denominations. While there has been some controversy related to northern and southern patterns of functioning, the major divisions in the church since reunion have reflected the fundamental liberal-conservative polarity. Similar polarities are found in all other mainline Protestant denominations and in other religious bodies as well.

The Focus of the Recent Struggles

Since the 1983 reunion, the focus of the struggles in the newly formed PC(USA) has been the ordination of what the 1978 UPCUSA General Assembly termed "self-affirming, practicing homosexuals." The terminology has changed over the years, but the issue remains the same: whether the Presbyterian Church will ordain as ministers of the Word and Sacrament, elders, or deacons members who are noncelibate, self-identified gay, lesbian, or transgender. The current position, included in the denomination's Constitution through amendment, is no.

A related matter is the blessing of same-sex unions. The official position on that issue, judicially determined and affirmed by the General Assembly, is no. Finally, the so-called Re-imagining God movement among some Presbyterian women (and men), resulting from a conference by that name held more than a decade ago, is generally included by conservatives among theological and ethical trends that they find deeply disturbing.

Most of the controversies that have embroiled the PC(USA) since 1983 have been waged in the higher governing bodies of the church—presbyteries, synods, and the General Assembly—though increasingly they are finding their way into individual congregations one way or another.

Thus, the oft-called Presbyterian wars of the last three decades have been largely limited to the ordained leadership of the PC(USA). Members of congregations have been much less aware or involved. Observers agree that most Presbyterians are somewhere in the middle of the theological spectrum, with the more extreme elements constituting a distinct minority.

The Theological Task Force on Peace, Unity, and Purity of the Church

The 213th General Assembly (2001) appointed the Theological Task Force on Peace, Unity, and Purity of the Church to take under consideration all that is dividing the church and to report back to the 217th General Assembly (2006) to be held in Birmingham, Alabama.

The task force report, together with recommendations, was issued on August 25, 2005, for churchwide study in preparation for consideration at the General Assembly.

The present volume, a collection of essays by thirteen Presbyterian leaders spanning the spectrum, was commissioned by Geneva Press to provide Presbyterians with an array of views on where the Presbyterian Church (U.S.A.) stands today and where it should be headed in the twenty-first century.

The editor believes that the thirteen contributors believe that God is calling the church to a new vision and to a new mission in the new century—one that will move the church beyond its obsession with sexuality issues and into a stronger witness to the gospel of Jesus Christ, not just among nations and peoples beyond our borders, but among the neighbors at our own doorstep. But contributors' analyses of the disorders that afflict us and their diagnoses for cure vary widely, as would be expected.

Decline of the Mainstream Denominations

Since the heady days of mid-twentieth-century Protestant religious hegemony in the United States, the mainstream denominations, among them the Presbyterians, have fallen on hard times. While rich in history, real estate, and assets, these denominations' collective strength is much diminished.

Denominations once thought to be the churches of the dispossessed have now moved into the mainstream, and the older, established churches, such as the Presbyterian, who trace their roots to the Colonial period have largely moved to the sideline in terms of numbers and influence in the culture.

In fact, Presbyterians since 1983 have been so preoccupied with reorganizing the machinery of their governance and fighting pitched battles over sexuality issues that they may not have noticed the enormous changes in the culture and their own ability to influence it in the name of Jesus Christ. Changes of the magnitude witnessed over the recent decades—the disestablishment, as it has been called, of mainline Protestantism—often go unnoticed until after they have occurred.

Far from being supportive of the church, the contemporary American culture outright opposes the deepest convictions of the historic Christian movement or, even worse, completely ignores them.

It could be argued that such a dramatic change is healthy for Presbyterians and other mainline Protestants, inasmuch as the church has always been the strongest—from the time of Jesus forward—when it was weakest.

Indeed, it may have taken this drastic turn of events to enable the triune God to get our attention, to bring new life and a new sense of mission to a relatively well-heeled group of quarreling Christians who collectively, at least, have been wandering in the wilderness for some time now.

At the heart of Reformed theology is the rock-solid belief in the sovereignty of God—over the whole creation, including the church. But for the will and purpose of God, the lordship of Jesus Christ, and the life given by the Holy Spirit, there would be no church. That the church of Jesus Christ thrives at any time or in any place is due solely to the grace and power of God. God's people may never lose hope for Christ's church. But sometimes, as now, hope for many is hard to sustain.

For those Presbyterians whose faith in Jesus Christ as Lord and Savior is strong, who imbibe deeply from the Holy Scriptures, who gather regularly to receive the Word and sacraments and to pray, who strive diligently in their own lives and the life of the world to bear witness to the gospel in word and deed—to these Presbyterian Christians—there is no fear about the future of the Presbyterian Church. They believe that the future is safely in God's hands. On the other hand, there is widespread frustration at the apparent disarray and loss of impetus.

Possible Futures for the PC(USA)

Any one of several outcomes can be imagined for the coming years, though our Lord prayed with his disciples on the eve of his crucifixion that they might all be one. Given the increasing splintering of the Christian church, the burden lies with any who would cause yet another schism.

God may choose to obliterate utterly the Presbyterian Church (U.S.A.) as we have known it for more than three hundred years; or to take the present company and revivify it in ways not yet seen; or to divide it up and deploy its subordinate components in different ways in different places for the sake of the coming kingdom; or to keep the fellowship together but configured in a much different way than we've known in the past. One thing everyone knows: the PC(USA) will be quite different in the coming years.

Keeping the PC(USA) together while gradually transforming the way we live together as one church may be the best for which we can hope in the twenty-first century. Several of the writers touch upon this new way of being the church together. The new church would be more attuned to Scripture and the pieties that have shaped previous generations; less corporate and bureaucratic in structure; more local, more familial, more missionally oriented; less dependent on money and real estate. Such a church could conceivably become a force to be reckoned with in the spiritually flabby culture that has evolved in postmodern America.

At the heart of such a church would be a love more God-like than is ordinarily displayed among factions in the PC(USA) today when dealing with one another.

Such a love would offer a compelling witness to a world that is looking for love in all the wrong places.

Such a love—for one another and for the world for which Jesus died and in which his body, the church, is called to live out its life under the sign of the cross—would be reminiscent of that found in the early church, which expanded exponentially in terms of numbers because of the power of the gospel.

Is there not a hunger abroad in the land for significant relationships, for authentic expressions of love that resemble what we Christians call agape, love that is free—like God's love—love that demands nothing in return, love that reaches out and includes all, rather than excluding many who do not somehow measure up, love that is unconditional?

Maybe Presbyterians by the grace of God and the power of Holy Spirit will be led into new ways of living together that will indeed constitute a radically new church whose witness to Jesus Christ as Lord and Savior will be strong and vibrant.

The Contributors

A word about this particular collection of writers is in order. It is indeed a stellar group.

This book is potentially of far greater significance than the events unfolding in 2006 in Birmingham with the gathering of the General Assembly to discuss, among other things, that which divides us so deeply, including ordination of self-identified, noncelibate gays and lesbians.

It is a remarkable collection of the mature reflections of some of the "best and the brightest" among us. The church thanks each writer who was willing to put himself or herself on the line, as it were, to further the peace, unity, and purity of the Presbyterian Church (U.S.A.) during this time of great controversy. The fact that these thirteen agreed to speak together in one volume offers a measure of hope for the future of the Presbyterian Church.

The Presbyterian Church (U.S.A.): A Mission in Progress

Clifton Kirkpatrick

A few years ago I had the good fortune of being invited to preach on the occasion of the two hundredth anniversary celebration of the First Presbyterian Church of Winchester, Virginia. I had been invited because the congregation remembered with fondness a former stated clerk of the General Assembly, Ashbel Green. Green was the stated clerk in the late 1700s when the assembly met in Winchester—before there was a Presbyterian church in that community. He vowed that one lasting contribution of that assembly would be the creation of a Presbyterian church in Winchester, and he gave major leadership to begin what is now the First Presbyterian Church. They had not had a stated clerk preach in that church since Ashbel Green. One of the elders opined in introducing me that "having a stated clerk visit once every two hundred years seems about right!"

That church, as you might imagine, had lived through many epochs in its ministry. It started as a rural congregation, became a church in the heart of a regional center in Virginia, lived through the Civil War and two world wars, and now is becoming a downtown church in a growing metropolitan region that is ministering to a postmodern, multicultural, multigenerational community in the Washington, D.C.–northern Virginia region. The church had reinvented its ministry many times over its two hundred years and was well aware that a new Reformation is in order for the twenty-first century. But the congregation was also equally aware that the church is founded on the "faith once delivered to the saints" and on the unchanging truths of the gospel of Jesus Christ.

They held dear the motto of our tradition, *Ecclesia reformata, semper reformanda* (a church reformed and always being reformed). They knew that change was the order of the day for ministry in the new situation in which they found themselves, but they also knew that such change must be based on the historic verities of the gospel and our Reformed tradition. So they adopted "A Mission in Progress" as the theme of their two hundredth anniversary celebration. They sought to use the occasion to mine their two-hundred-year tradition for the abiding truths about God and the church to serve as a foundation for the new ministry to which they were being called in twenty-first-century northern Virginia.

They had it right! Their theme could well be the theme of the Presbyterian Church (U.S.A.) as a whole as we seek to do ministry in the twenty-first century. We too are celebrating major anniversaries in our life together. In 2003, we celebrated the twentieth anniversary of our latest reunion into the Presbyterian Church (U.S.A.), and in 2006 we will celebrate the three hundredth anniversary of the creation of the first presbytery on this side of the Atlantic, which marks the founding of American Presbyterianism. We also face a new missionary situation that calls the church again to new Reformation. If we are to be a vital church in twenty-first-century America, major changes will have to take place.

This volume of essays attempts to offer resources for Presbyterians to be faithful in addressing both sides of the coin—discovering where God is calling us to a new Reformation and, at the same time, reminding us of the core values of the Reformed tradition on which that new Reformation needs to be built. You will find in the pages that follow wisdom from my colleagues about places where God is calling us Presbyterians to a new Reformation and resources from our Reformed tradition to be faithful to that call. I want to use this introduction to share with you a summary of the core values of our Reformed tradition, which are an anchor for the renewal of the church in this age and in any age.

At the time of our most recent reunion into the Presbyterian Church (U.S.A.), the General Assembly and the presbyteries approved a new *Book of Order* with a unique feature. It had what one might expect of books of order in terms of rules, procedures, and policies to govern the church. However, the innovation was a beautiful summary of the core values and deepest beliefs of Presbyterian and Reformed Christians, which is found at the very beginning of the *Book of Order* (the first four chapters). These chapters outline the unique gifts of the Reformed tradition and are the foundation for "what the church needs" for its renewal and reformation in any age.

While I encourage you to explore anew these chapters, I also want to use this essay to lift out ten jewels of the Reformed tradition, which are the treasure of these chapters and the core values around which any new Reformation needs to be centered:

Jesus Christ Is the Living Head of the Church

For Reformed Christians, there is no doubt about who is the head of the church. It is not a bishop or a pope, a pastor or a session—or even the "pillar of the church" who has been there from the very beginning of a congregation. It is Jesus Christ! As the *Book of Order* makes clear, "Christ calls the church into being, giving it all that is necessary for its mission in the world, for its building up, and for its service to God" (*Book of Order*, G-1.0100b). A faithful church is always a Christ-centered church!

The Great Ends of the Church Are Our Foundational Calling

A century ago, one of our predecessor denominations, the United Presbyterian Church of North America, adopted a foundational purpose statement for the church and its congregations called the Great Ends of the Church. While its language shows its age, its vision is timeless. Those Great Ends are in our *Book of Order* as the purpose statement for our church:

> The great ends of the church are the proclamation of the gospel for the salvation of humankind; the shelter, nurture, and spiritual fellowship of the children of God; the maintenance of divine worship; the preservation of the truth; the promotion of social righteousness; and the exhibition of the Kingdom of Heaven to the world. (*B.O.*, G-1.0200)

To be a faithful Presbyterian Church (or a faithful Presbyterian!) is to be engaged in a mission that is holistic: proclaiming the gospel and working for social justice, nurturing the children of God (within and without the church) and upholding God's truth, worshipping God with gusto and living the Christian life.

We Are a People of the Book and the Books

While we affirm that Jesus Christ is the head of the church and the Word of God, we are also a people with a high view of Scripture and the confessions. We believe that Scripture is the authoritative witness, without parallel, to God's saving action in Jesus Christ. As such, the Bible should be at the center of our lives as Christians. As Reformed Christians we also value the historic confessions of the church, through which Christians in various ages have lifted up biblical truth both for their own time and for all time. We are convinced that the best way to know the truth of God is not to be focused only on the "here and now," but to be open to the witness of those throughout the ages who have experienced God's saving grace in their time, and in doing so to glean the eternal truths of the gospel.

We Affirm the Faith of the Church Catholic

Presbyterians do not have a "corner on the gospel," but rather share with all Christians certain foundational convictions about the Christian faith. With all Christians we affirm the Trinity and the incarnation as foundational doctrines. We invite all baptized Christians to join us at the Lord's Table. The confessions we repeat more than any others in affirmations of faith during our worship services are the universal creeds of all Christian churches: the Apostles' Creed and the Nicene Creed.

We Embrace the Great Truths of the Protestant Reformation

While we share our faith and affirm our unity with all Christians, we as Reformed Christians clearly locate ourselves as a church of the Protestant Reformation. The rallying cry of the Reformation, *sola gratia, sola fide, sola scriptura* (grace alone, faith alone, Scripture alone), is our basic orientation toward the Christian life. We hold to the "priesthood of all believers" and to the scriptural promise of salvation by the grace of God in Jesus Christ, which we can never earn but can freely receive through faith in Christ.

The Sovereignty of God Is the Great Theological Distinctive of the Reformed Tradition

The special contribution of Reformed Christians to the Reformation was the focus on the sovereignty of God. Because God is sovereign over all of life—and not just the church or our private spiritual lives—Presbyterians have always sought to witness to God's justice in the world, to build up our churches as covenant communities, to exercise faithful stewardship, and to joyfully receive our election as being not just for our salvation but also to enable us to serve God and others. Because of our confidence in the sovereignty of God, we can also look to the future with hope and creativity because we know the future is in God's hands.

The Church Is a Missionary Society

For John Calvin there were two "marks of the church": the Word rightly preached and the sacraments rightly administered. Wherever this happened, Calvin felt there was a true church. John Knox in Scotland added a third mark, that of discipline or nurture. In the twentieth century there has been a fourth "mark of the church" that most Reformed Christians have come to affirm, that the church is a missionary society. We have been called to faith and to life in the church not for ourselves, but to be a faithful expression of God's mission in the world. That is why a core element of Presbyterian churches everywhere is our commitment to mission, sharing the gospel in word and deed both where we live and around the world.

To Be Presbyterian Is to Be Ecumenical

Presbyterians have never understood themselves to be "the church" but rather to be one part of the church, which God intends to be one. That is why Presbyterians are always leaders in the ecumenical movement. We are a people who share Jesus' deepest yearning that we "all may be one . . . that the world may believe" (John 17:21).

The Church of Jesus Christ Is an Inclusive Church

The biblical image of the body of Christ (1 Corinthians 12) has always been powerful for Presbyterians. We are a people who believe that diversity in our world (just as in our bodies) is a gift of God and that the church is a place where all people should be welcomed and affirmed. There is no place in the church of Jesus Christ for discriminating against or marginalizing people because of gender, race, sexual orientation, physical limitations, or marital status.

How We Govern Ourselves Is a Witness to the World

It is no accident that our church is named after its polity. (The word "presbyterian" is derived from the Greek word for elder!). We believe in the priesthood of all believers, in the shared leadership of ministers of the Word and Sacrament and elders, and in the discernment of God's will through solemn assemblies where the elected spiritual leaders "are not simply to reflect the will of the people, but rather to seek together to find and represent the will of Christ" (*B.O.*, G-4.0301d). At its best, this form of decision making enables the church to be a "provisional demonstration of what God intends for all of humanity" (*B.O.*, G-3.0200).

Conclusion

The house in which we live in the Presbyterian Church (U.S.A.) clearly needs to be renovated, and major parts need to be rebuilt, if we are to be an effective missionary church in the twenty-first century. However, our foundation in the Reformed tradition is firm. In fact, it is this foundation and these core values that free us up to be a missionary church in the twenty-first century.

Like the faithful people in the First Presbyterian Church in Winchester, Virginia, I hope that all of our churches will seek to be churches that are reforming as well as seeking to be reformed. A new Reformation and a new reclaiming of our roots in the Reformed tradition are indeed two sides of the same coin—a coin of great value for the renewal of the Presbyterian Church (U.S.A.) as a vital Reformed church for the twenty-first century.

Ecclesia Reformata, Semper Reformanda: Reformed and Always to Be Reformed

Anna Case-Winters

Contemporary Use and Misuse

Ecclesia reformata, semper reformanda! Even to this day, these ancient words are a rallying cry for us, a motto that reminds us of who we are and who we intend to be. But what does this phrase really mean? It is used as a springboard in all kinds of contexts and conversations, sometimes with little sense of how it arose and what it meant among those who first used it in the aftermath of the sixteenth-century Reformation. It is appropriated in times of disagreement and pressed into the service of our own agendas, even sometimes wielded as a weapon against those who differ from us, as if to say, "My position is more Reformed than your position!" Then we have the moral advantage.

This is a misuse and probably also a misunderstanding of its meaning. Indeed, this saying should be a watchword for us, but we need a heightened sense of its meaning and the challenge it puts before us. Used without attentiveness to its historical context and import, it loses much of its power to challenge us.

Historical Clarifications and Corrections

Our Reformed motto, rightly understood, challenges both the conservative and the liberal impulses that characterize our diverse body today. For it does not bless either preservation for preservation's sake, or change for change's sake. In the sixteenth-century context, the impulse it reflected was neither liberal nor conservative but radical, in the sense of returning to the "root." What the Reformers believed was that the church had become corrupt, so change was needed, but it was a change in the interest of preservation and restoration

This article, in an edited version, was published in the May 2004 issue of *Presbyterians Today*, 100 Witherspoon St., Louisville, KY 40202-1396. Appreciation is expressed to the publisher and to the writer for permission to use it in this book.

of more authentic faith and life—a church reformed and always to be reformed according to the word of God.

Interestingly, the actual saying is not forged in the more adventurous sixteenth century, first wave of the Reformation, but rather in the context of seventeenth-century Protestant orthodoxy. The actual origin of this particular form of the formula is uncertain, but it and similar formulations appear about this time. One of the early forms, *ecclesia reformanda quia reformata* ("the church to be reformed because it has been reformed") is found in the writings of a Dutch Reformed theologian, Gisbertus Voetius (1589–1676). There the concern was for the centrality of Scripture in guiding right doctrine and right practice.

In the polemic of the Reformation, the Reformers were urgent to make the claim of "antiquity," for the cultural assumption of the day was that what is older is better. This is strange to our contemporary ears, for we do not share this assumption. If anything, we applaud the new and "innovative." But one of the serious charges church authorities hurled at the Reformers was that they were "innovating." Calvin responded to this and other charges in his treatise on "The Necessity of Reforming the Church." As he put it, "we are accused of rash and impious innovation, for having ventured to propose any change at all on the former state of the Church" (p. 185). He then goes on to counter that they were not "innovating." Rather, they were restoring the church to its true nature, purified from the "innovations" that riddled the church through centuries of inattention to Scripture and theological laxity. The appeal was to a more ancient source, Scripture—*sola scriptura* (Scripture alone). By submitting themselves to Scripture, the churches of the Reformation movement were purging themselves of these unwanted "innovations" and returning to more ancient and therefore purer forms of church life (Steinmetz, p. 459).

Given this context, using the motto to back up any and all "innovations" would be a misuse of the original intent. In many places where the slogan appears, the phrase is completed with a clarifying addition so that it reads: *ecclesia reformata, semper reformanda secundum verbum dei*, which translates, "reformed and always being reformed according to the Word of God." Reform, where it is advocated, must find its grounding here.

Another potential misuse is lodged in a common mistranslation. Sometimes the phrase is mistranslated as "reformed and always reforming." This can mislead us to believe that the church is the agent of its own reformation. God is the agent of reformation. The church is rather the object of God's reforming work. God's agency and initiative have priority here. The Latin verb is in fact passive and is much better translated as "always being reformed" or "always to be reformed." Professor Harold Nebelsick put it well: "We are the recipients of the activity of the Holy Spirit which reforms the church in accordance with the Word of God" (p. 62). The church is God's church, a creature of God's Word and Spirit. As we say in our Brief Statement of Faith in the *Book of Confessions* (10.1), "We belong to God." God's Word and Spirit guide the church's forming and reforming.

The *Book of Order*, in chapter 2, on "The Church and Its Confessions" (G-2.0200), follows the mistranslation, but is on target with its theological interpretation. It states: "The church, in obedience to Jesus Christ, is open to the reform of its standards of doctrine as well as of governance. The church affirms 'Ecclesia reformata, semper reformanda,' that is, 'the church reformed, always reforming,' according to the Word of God and the call of the Spirit." That last phrase is crucial in clarifying both the direction (and the Director!) of the church's reform.

Theological Foundations of Openness "to Be Reformed"

Part of our openness to be reformed comes out of a conviction about *who we are*. Reformed folk have been particularly aware of human fallibility and sinfulness. One of the particular/peculiar gifts of our tradition is the notion of "total depravity." It is one of our least understood gifts to the ecumenical community, but all it means is that we recognize that no aspect of our lives is unaffected by our estrangement from God. Even our best endeavors and highest aspirations are prone to sin and error. Forms of faith and life in the church are no exception. This is why Reformed confessions tend to have their own built-in disclaimers. The preface to the Scots Confession invites all readers to offer correction from Scripture if they find the confession to be in error. The Westminster Confession of Faith (*Book of Confessions*, 6.175) asserts that synods and councils "may err, and many have erred."

We acknowledge that the church, even at is best, is a frail and fallible human institution. We know that we "hold these treasures in earthen vessels." It might be said that reform is the institutional counterpart of repentance (Dowey, p. 11). Recognizing how far short we fall from God's intentions, we continually submit all doctrines and structures to be reformed according to the Word of God and the call of the Spirit. The church is a frail and fallible pilgrim people, a people on the way, who are not yet what we shall be. The church, because of who we are, remains open to always being reformed.

Openness to be reformed comes not only because of who we are but because of *who God is*. The God "whom alone we worship and serve" (Brief Statement of Faith, *B.C.*, 10. 1) is a living God. As the Reformed theologian Karl Barth expressed it, God is the One who loves in freedom. God is not bound, either to our tradition or to our particular contemporary context. God's revelation is ever a gift, never a given.

As Professor Edward Dowey rightly observed, "Reform has a backward and a forward reference. It leads not only back to the Bible but also forward under the word" (Dowey, p. 10). The Confession of 1967 underscores this teaching, "As God has spoken [God's] word in diverse cultural situations, the church is confident that [God] will continue to speak through the Scriptures in a changing world and in every form of human culture" (*B.C.*, 9.29).

The backward and forward reference of reform invites us, on the one hand, to attend respectfully to the wisdom and scriptural interpretations of those who have gone before us with humility. On the other hand, it pushes us to do more than simply reiterate what our fathers and mothers in the faith have said. Rather, we must do in our day what they did in theirs: worship and serve the living God. Therefore, while we honor the forms of faith and life that have been bequeathed to us, we honor them best in a spirit of openness to the Word and the Spirit that formed and continues to re-form the church. The church, *because of who God is*—a Living God, who loves in freedom—remains open to always being reformed.

Contemporary Meanings

A vision of the church reformed and always being reformed is one of the gifts the Reformed have to bring to the wider Christian church. There are intimations that such a notion may already be out there among our ecumenical partners. A case in point would be one of the memorable moments at the first-ever face-to-face conversation between the Presbyterian Church (U.S.A.) and the Roman Catholic Church, represented by the Pontifical Council for the Promotion of Christian Unity. Cardinal Cassidy observed, "You have a saying that seems to be at the heart of your self-understanding as a church. What do you mean when you keep referring in your documents to *ecclesia reformata, semper reformanda?*" It was a moving moment to hear as the twelve Presbyterians at the table sought to say in their own words what that means to us. It became all the more moving when the Roman Catholic representatives called our attention to the papal encyclical *Unitatis Redintegratio* in which they have now said, in the strongest way possible, that the church is continually in need of reform. This was a high point of the dialogue. It may be that the call to be reformed—while it remains our distinctive gift—is no longer our exclusive possession.

Ecclesia reformata, semper reformanda. This motto calls us to something more radical than we have imagined. It challenges both liberal and conservative impulses and the habits and agendas we have fallen into lately. It brings a prophetic critique to our cultural accommodation—either to the past or to the present—and calls us to communal and institutional repentance. It invites us, as people who worship and serve a living God, to be open to being "re-formed" according to the Word of God and the call of the Spirit.

What the Presbyterian Church (U.S.A.) Needs Today: Thirteen Views

Chapter 1

A Deeply Engraved People

Richard Ray

*I*t was not a year that we have grown up hearing about. It was 1688. Not many people, either then or now, would have paid much attention to two passing events. One was the death of John Bunyan. Among other books, he had published *Grace Abounding to the Chief of Sinners* in 1666 and *The Pilgrim's Progress* in 1678.

John Bunyan

John Bunyan died leaving these penetrating accounts of spiritual struggle. The Puritan convictions that had guided his thought and shaped his message were already self-evident to many Christians at odds with the Church of England. These included the central authority of the Scriptures and the continuing power of the life, death, and resurrection of Jesus Christ to overcome evil and to renew our lives. Bunyan had been sent to jail for twelve years, largely on his insistence that *The Book of Common Prayer* was not scriptural and his practice of preaching outside of the established church. In all such issues, Bunyan had believed that his chief adversary was not the church.

The reform of the church was a secondary matter. The primary issue was explicitly spiritual. And until people faced this issue, nothing else about the church could be amended. Had Bunyan himself not heard Satan needle him, "I shall be too hard for you, I will cool you insensibly, by degrees, by little and little . . . though I be seven years in chilling your heart . . . I shall have you cold before long" (*Grace Abounding to the Chief of Sinners* [London: Penguin Books, 1987], 30)?

The Wesleys

The second event of 1688 would have seemed even more ordinary. It marked, however, the beginning of something quite different. It was Samuel and Susanna Wesley's wedding day. Who would have guessed that of their nineteen

3

children John and Charles would become leaders of history's greatest evangelical revival from within the Church of England? John Wesley's literary production, counting his sermons and his letters, far exceeded the books of Bunyan. And the hymns of John's brother Charles have enriched the life of the church forever.

John Locke

The following year saw another, quite different event that would shape English life. John Locke, living in Holland for a time and writing to a theologian in Amsterdam, outlined his views concerning the growing religious pluralism back home in England. Published in 1689, *A Letter Concerning Toleration* (Library of Liberal Arts, Indianapolis: Bobbs-Merrill, 1950) provided what many came to see as a wise and insightful appreciation for the separate governance of church and state.

As we read it today, we appreciate the understandable concern that civil government should not interfere in religious matters. The background to it, however, was more complex. It reflected the growing nonchalance of the educated elite toward organized religion. Church leaders were soon following the scientists and philosophers in their belief that human reason would before long enable them to decide all-important matters. Reason was considered to be the reliable guide for sifting out doctrinal fine points and for arriving at a mellow, self-evident sort of faith. Scripture was still read in the churches, but thoughtful people were less likely to rely upon it for spiritual authority in their lives. And church officials, protecting their ties with the cultural leaders, were leaning closer to the deist philosophy. It was good to be thought well of in high places. The urgency of the Reformation was over. The biblical account of the decisive, unpredictable, and interfering God that fired the imagination of Bunyan and the Wesleys was being diminished.

The rational order of Isaac Newton's universe, the ritual conformity in church, and a comfortable sense of latitude with regard to the moral law seemed to be quite enough. It provided a religion without authoritative demand. Christianity was increasingly considered to be a civilized and sensible practice. And the ministers of the church, particularly those who had found favor with ecclesiastical superiors, came to hold a comfortable niche.

However, when it comes to spiritual matters, things are quite different. Great things often have small beginnings. On the evening of May 24, 1738, John Wesley attended a small prayer meeting of dissidents. He heard words read from the Preface to Luther's *Commentary on Romans*, and this turned out to be all that he needed. He felt a sense of warmth in his heart and a personal assurance that his sins were forgiven. When he awoke the next morning, Wesley knew that Christ was now real to him in a different way. "All my strength," he would write, "lay in keeping my eyes fixed on him" (Robert G. Tuttle Jr., *John Wesley: His Life and Theology* [Grand Rapids: Zondervan, 1978], 200).

The Situation Today

None of this, of course, is very different from our situation today. As Presbyterians, long used to a sense of order and tradition, we have come to accept certain things. Our spiritual vitality comes to us through family ties, stable programs, predictable worship, and a comforting belief that secular culture is our friend. Yet whenever a Bunyan or a Wesley appears, stirring up an unfamiliar sense of immediacy and enthusiasm, a fissure begins to appear. We become aware that they and their company are different. They talk of conversion, but we talk about confirmation and commitment. They talk of evangelism, but we prefer to talk about new church development. They speak of a riveting sense of immediacy, and we are more comfortable with Locke's concept of the gradual "inward and full persuasion of the mind" (quoted in W. R. Sorley, *A History of British Philosophy to 1900* [Cambridge, 1965], 126). They exercise a marked sense of freedom and simplicity with regard to liturgical outfits and practices, and we are increasingly oriented to stoles and rote responses.

One wonders. Could a Bunyan or a Wesley come to his electrifying sense of spiritual reality and inward peace while serving on the Christian education committee with us? Their experiences of an intervening Spirit and of daunting supernatural struggles are as alien to most of us as they would have been to the Latitudinarian circle known to Locke and Wesley at Oxford or the so-called Cambridge Platonists who, at about the same time, sought a gentler style of spirituality. To speak in Bunyan's terms, if he were here with us, would he have occasionally wondered if he were being spiritually "cooled"? And would Wesley have asked if anyone known to us had ever had an experience like his, or had come to a deep and abiding sense of personal assurance directly from the Lord?

Spiritual Deadness

Spiritual incursions and gifts of personal clarity are relatively rare in our churches today. They aren't reported regularly. In fact, when we occasionally read the verse found at 1 Samuel 3:1, "The word of the LORD was rare in those days; visions were not widespread," we wonder if the verse is also talking about us.

Even if personal assurance about faith is rarely reported in dramatic terms, a true vein of dedication and sacrifice runs deep within many of our churches.

We are noted for getting good things done in good order. Presbyterian hammers have built many Habitat homes. Presbyterian Meals on Wheels have fed many who would have been hungry, and mission partnerships with distant congregations have sprung up everywhere. And when it comes to Scripture, if you look in our pew racks or in our classrooms, you will likely see plenty of Bibles there.

Institutional Decline

Yet, in spite of so much, there is a sense of uncertainty. Offerings to support the denomination's missions are down, the membership tally has shrunk, people report that they have difficulty in explaining to others what they believe about Christ, and a feeling of ambiguity seems to hang over the governance of the church. The average age of the members gives the impression that young adults are beginning to wander away. Circling around all of this, Bunyan and Wesley might ask, "You folks are nice, but do you really have a sense of authority in your lives?"

We know that we are not alone. People who late in life become spiritual shakers and movers often reported bouts of near clinical fatigue when they were young. Chronic depression seems to be a prerequisite for spiritual insight in due time. When we walk through the pages of George Fox's *Journal* or Teresa of Avila's *Autobiography*, we wonder how they managed to survive. John Bunyan's and John Wesley's early years certainly seemed marked by what their own practitioners called melancholia. And if someone tested us Presbyterians for optimism, we might come out, despite our claims to the contrary, ambivalent at best.

The Encouraging Mystery

The encouraging thing is that spiritual leaders often seem to have been motivated by a providentially inspired restlessness when they were young. They were discontented. Their search for spiritual conviction was too painful to have been entirely their own invention. The Spirit seems to drive us nearly to distraction for a time. God still favors the wilderness—and those renewal wilderness journeys later called exiles—to humble his people. Perhaps we Presbyterians have been touched by some of this. As Morton Kelsey puts it, in spite of our relative material security, many people are anxious about the mysterious loss of personal meaning in their lives (*Discernment: A Study in Ecstasy and Evil* [New York: Paulist Press, 1978], 13).

From a prophetic perspective, the encouraging thing is that God may have intentionally led us into a place where we will have to listen for him again.

What About the Presbyterians?

Presbyterians are good talkers. We spend a lot of time listening to ourselves. One of the temptations that comes from being clever is that we want our pronouncements, our liturgies, and our scholarship to be better than the best. We also have a sense of proper things. We can tell when all of the external requirements have been met. We are experts at that. So what are we to think when some of us have had enough and seem bored and wander off to pursue other things? We look at ourselves and wonder if God's mark still rests on us.

For most of us, being Presbyterian is still better than many other things. Some of us have tried other denominations and ended up here by choice. Others have deep family roots. Whatever the case, we still wish that we knew how to hold out our half-empty cups of faith and have them filled again. We realize that the Puritan worldview that guided Bunyan and the Moravian movement that touched Wesley are not as easily available to us today. But, being Presbyterian, we may still find more to help us than we had thought. After all—and we should remember this—the covenant is still intact.

The Central Role of Scripture

The spiritual circumstances that concerned our early Swiss Reformers, John Calvin and his earlier contemporary, Huldrych Zwingli, would be familiar to us. The labels would be different, but the underlying problems would be the same. To put their situation in our terms, they did not know whom they could trust. They were concerned that church leaders were pursuing their own pet causes. They felt the Scripture had been submerged under recent ideologies, and they longed to restore both confidence and self-discipline to their congregations. And when they entered worship services, they sensed that "the word of the LORD was rare in those days" (1 Samuel 3:1). There was no certain trumpet to be heard.

Then they began to spend more concentrated time—to use our words, quality time—with Scripture. They did not just peek into it for their daily devotions, or chop it up into liturgically correct lectionary segments, or spend time getting their exegetical interpretations technically correct. They were not content simply to repeat the interpretations that they had always heard. They dallied over it and stuck with the difficult parts until unexpected things began to happen. Scripture becomes strange before it becomes familiar again.

You have to live with the text. We assume that Scripture is sound, inspired by God, profitable for teaching, and the basis for our church. We accept it too easily; before long we begin to realize that it is telling us what we want it to say. The key to reading Scripture is that we have to listen to it until we no longer know what we once thought we did. We have to take off our shoes, as it were. Only then are we ready to hear God speak.

The Presbyterian way to rid ourselves of the Presbyterian illness is to return to Scripture with a new commitment. It is a simple but taxing procedure. It takes time. And Calvin, who becomes our spiritual physician once more, reveals in his major work, *The Institutes of the Christian Religion*, how much time it cost him. He read Scripture, but he did not read it alone. Even as one who spent time with it privately, he took with him the voices of others. There are many citations of other writers in his book. There are seven hundred references to Augustine alone. This shows that the great writers in our own tradition may have more to teach us than the popular gurus to whom we look for help all too often.

It still takes a Presbyterian physician to cure a Presbyterian soul. Calvin tells us in Book 3 of the *Institutes* that when we dig into Scripture itself a miracle far beyond our control can occur. He called it the inner witness of the Holy Spirit, and he intended for his readers to grasp that he was referring to a very real and personal experience. It is an experience, he wrote, leaving the testimony to Christ "engraved like a seal upon our hearts" (3.1.1). And our feelings, in this instance, provide the clue to a deeper change that has been miraculously set in motion. The words in the text itself penetrate and influence our character. In the process, they provide a depth and certainty of conviction, an assurance, that can enable us to take the offense against the cultural forces that frighten us. In this type of study, the outcome is not merely a warmed heart or a sense of victory over evil. It is more. It guides us into a spirited union with Christ himself. It thus becomes a uniquely organic wisdom. We grow, as Calvin put it, "into one body with him." And it occurs as we "climb higher" than conventional brainpower can enable us to climb, until we "examine the secret energy of the Spirit."

At this point, says Calvin, a deeply personal cauterization or "cleansing" occurs. The creative power of God engraves his truth in the sealing words of Scripture, as a heated signet is pressed deeply into molten wax. Christ is welded as a living transplant into our hearts. We are never alone. Nor need we ever be afraid.

Calvin put it like this even in speaking of the Old Testament patriarchs:

That firm certainty of doctrine was engraved in their hearts, so that they were convinced and even understood that what they had learned proceeded from God. For by his Word God rendered faith unambiguous forever, a faith that should be superior to all opinions. This is the inner knowledge which alone quickens dead souls. (1.6.1, 2)

What all could Calvin have included in his concept of "dead souls"? It would be hard to say. Would it include Bunyan's wariness of being "cooled"? When I read over the extensive list of books that Wesley read as a young man, I am unsure whether or not in that context, it represents one who was driven by a sense of intellectual panic. What does seem to be puzzling is the concept of toleration. It seems to be more relevant to social freedom than to doctrinal issues.

Toleration

Are those who are rock solid in their own beliefs free to be tolerant of the views of others? Or does it work in the reverse? Perhaps it is sometimes like this—when we become less certain of our own beliefs, we begin to speak more frequently of being open and tolerant of all opinions. We feel that there may be, in the final analysis, no worthwhile claim to final truth.

Historically, the time had come for John Locke and for a new sense of intellectual tolerance. Nevertheless, it is notable that as Locke left his own Puritan background behind, he became personally interested in the question of tolerance. And is our current intellectual environment now reflected in that distant mirror? The current breadth of personal beliefs heard across our church certainly suggests that doctrinal consensus is hard to find. It lifts the historical Presbyterian tolerance for "scruples" to a new level.

It does seem evident that when the established church in England on the one hand became characterized by theological latitude and on the other hand tightened down in its liturgical conformity, spontaneous souls like Bunyan and Wesley broke loose. The interior experiences could no longer be contained. Toleration in this context was less a reflection of ambiguity than the social condition in which very strong, fresh opinions could be reasserted.

What will then become of us as we feel the divine engraver reaching his hand down to touch our hearts? We do not have the power to know the answer to that. We are only assured that the authority of the inner witness of the Holy Spirit to the word points toward something far more expansive than we have dared to trust. John Bunyan and John Wesley encountered it. John Calvin described it for us; almost always reluctant to tell us much about his own experience, in his definitive work he instructed us in it. Perhaps he would have overreached his own commitment to Scripture if he had attempted to say more.

"A Deeply Engraved People"

Our reconstruction in grace does lead us to both the grandeur and the humility of this. We are a deeply engraved people. We are engraved with Scripture by the Spirit and virtually welded into Christ. Our existence is contained within this claim upon us. And that is what Scripture means by the covenant.

Caught within history's incongruities and paradoxes, we are by faith what we cannot yet be in fact. We are engraved by grace, if not yet fully transformed by grace. And this provides us with the recklessness to obey a call that we could never have claimed to discern fully. Being engraved in this way we are triply marked by Father, Son, and Holy Spirit. This mark tells us who we are in multiple ways that we could never discern on our own and gives us back the point of identity that the ravages of history often threaten to take from us.

After delivering these concepts as a sermon at a nearby convent, Zwingli developed them into a book, *On the Clarity and Certainty of the Word of God*. It is the clarity by which we live, even though it always remains elusive, humbling, searching, and frequently driving us into the wilderness we would not choose. And it is here in our wilderness that the text, whatever its history and form, becomes the sharper, cutting edge for our mind. We are deeply engraved with the words that become more mysterious as time passes. We are not cooled. Our engraved spirit always remains hot. For the One who engraves never slumbers or sleeps.

Questions for Discussion

1. What does the author mean by the word "engraved"?
2. Do Presbyterians have difficulty in expressing their faith passionately?
3. Is it possible or likely that Presbyterians will once again become known as the "people of the book"—the Bible? How important is Bible study in the life of your congregation? Your own life?

Chapter 2

The Power of Paradox

Susan Andrews

*O*nce upon a time there was a young seeker who was confused. She didn't know where to find God. And so after several years of wandering, she sought out a wise and seasoned saint. "Tell me, sir," she said. "Please tell me where I can find God." After a moment's hesitation, the old man reached out a hand and responded, "Follow me." The seasoned saint and the curious seeker traveled through the woods and across some fields until they reached a cold, deep stream. At this point, the old man waded into the water and invited the curious one to join him. Soon the surprised seeker was next to him, and the saint pushed her young head under the water. Before long, the student began to squirm and resist the water, but the old man maintained firm and gentle pressure. The moments passed and the thrashing beneath the water became more intense. Finally, in desperation and with a great surge of passion, the seeker reared up out of the water, devouring great gasps of air and sputtering furiously at the old saint. When she had calmed down, the old man spoke, "My child, when you want God as much as you wanted air, it is then that you will find God."[1]

In these troubled times in the Presbyterian Church (U.S.A.), we are having a hard time finding God. And one of the reasons is that we are concentrating on the where, instead of the how. Since God has already found us, our task is not to seek, but to yearn—to find ways to open our hearts to the presence of God already in our midst. In our battles over the authority and interpretation of Scripture, we are trying to find God in the fine print of the written word. In our polity struggles to win influence in and among governing bodies, we are trying to find God in the architecture of structure. And in our bitter bickering

Portions of this chapter are adapted from Susan R. Andrews, "Agony, Passion, and Hope: The Future of the Presbyterian Church, A Pastor's Perspective," published by McCormick Theological Seminary, Office of Seminary Relations, May 1991.

about abortion and homosexuality, about the true meaning of evangelism and social witness policy, we are trying to find God in doctrine and law. In concentrating on the where—instead of the how—we end up putting God in boxes, and compartmentalizing ourselves as well. And we miss the God who has already found us.

In the story of the curious seeker, it was the wanting instead of the worrying, the process instead of the product, the journey instead of the jargon, that helped her find the Holy. It was the way that led to the where. In fact, the way became the where. The biblical story often makes the same point. It was through old-age bitterness that Sarah found God. It was through cave depression that Elijah found God. It was through pregnant waiting that Mary found God. It was through wilderness temptation that Jesus found God. It was through physical suffering that Paul found God. For all of them it was the way that became the where—a way that became inevitably filled with both power and passion, a way filled with emotional, as well as intellectual, changes.

In order to find God, we, as part of sidelined, disempowered American mainline Protestantism, must discover and embrace a Presbyterian Way—the particular Way that God becomes flesh in the body of the Presbyterian Church. How we look for God will determine whether or not we find God through the particularity of a Presbyterian lens—and whether or not that lens will be focused enough for all the world to see.

The Uniqueness of the Presbyterian Way

So, what is the Presbyterian Way? What is particularly powerful and passionate about the way we find God? A few years ago I was talking to a couple in our congregation—two professional economists who worked for the World Bank. He is British—a dropout from the Anglican Church. She is Filipino—a guilt-ridden graduate of Presbyterian mission efforts in Manila.

They had been hanging around the edges of the congregation for a year, only because their eighth-grade son kept asking about God. Who is God? Where is God? How do I find God? The parents were at a loss, because they had totally misplaced their own sense of God. From the perspective of their high-powered, intellectualized, economically focused lives, they were not sure that the God of their childhood even exists.

The mother, especially, was miserable. She had found an evangelical Bible study that met during lunch at the World Bank (of all places!), and she was trying in vain to find the Spirit. She listened to stories of impassioned conversions and miracle cures and kept waiting for the warmth of God to overpower her life. Instead, all she felt was doubt and guilt and emptiness.

Her husband, on the other hand, was trying to find God in the rituals of worship, the only handles he had been given within the Anglican tradition of his youth. As pleasing as they are, the songs and stories and sacraments of worship failed to reveal to him the clear and convincing face of God.

As I listened to their angst and their yearning, I began to understand why this couple was sitting eating omelets in the fellowship hall of a fairly liberal Presbyterian church. In the providence and wisdom of God's grace, they were being led to this part of God's family, because for them the Presbyterian Way may well be the only way they will find God.

We talked, then, about the value of healthy agnosticism, about the appropriateness of journey as a metaphor of faith, about conversion as a process instead of an event, about doubt as a vital nutrient for faith, about intellectual curiosity as a channel of the Spirit, about God living in the midst of the secular morass of global economic policy, about the necessity of moral struggle within the ambiguous ethics of upper-middle-class living. Looking for God in the seeming absence of God is the place where this couple found themselves, and their vague hunger was God's call to them. The Presbyterian Way—of worshipping, studying, questioning, integrating—became the way for their hunger to be filled.

I am a lifelong Presbyterian, the daughter and granddaughter of Presbyterian pastors. My earliest memories of church are crawling around under the pews in dozens of Presbyterian churches while my mother spoke and sang and ran meetings in her myriad roles within Presbyterial and Synodical.

Going to church was the central rhythm of my life. Sunday school was as much a habit as brushing my teeth. I loved worship, even when I didn't understand it, because I felt wrapped in a holy presence. As I got older and began to sense the politics of the church—the arguments and tensions within the church, the inevitable conflicts between my father and the leaders of the church—I began to understand sin in an existential way. Though this knowledge confused me, it also comforted me. As I got in touch with my own imperfections and needs, it felt good to be part of a community where being less than perfect was okay.

I take you on this detour into nostalgia only because my story is very much a Presbyterian story. In seminary, when I finally admitted that God was calling me into parish ministry, I went on a denominational treasure hunt: Episcopalians, Congregationalists, Unitarians, Jews. I explored lots of alien territory. But the roots were too strong. The Presbyterian Way of disciplined spirit, of judicious justice, of careful glory, of scholarly emotion, of embarrassed piety, of passionate polity, of wonder-filled worship—it was the only way that could become my way. What I found unique about Presbyterianism on my treasure hunt, I still find unique today.

Four Paradoxes of the Presbyterian Way

At the heart of the Presbyterian Way are the paradoxes of the Reformed faith. We no longer live in a dualistic world—an either/or world. Rather, in the complexity of God's sovereign grace we are called to embrace the tensions of a both/and world. Four particular paradoxes seem relevant these days.

1. *Order and ardor.* While serving as moderator of the 215th General Assembly (2003–2004), I had the privilege of traveling to South Africa. One Sunday morning we traveled to Alexandria, one of the black townships outside Johannesburg. As we entered the muddy streets, we saw barefoot children walking amid sewage and garbage, and thousands of tin shacks jammed together stretched as far as the eye could see.

But then we entered the simple brick walls of the new Presbyterian church, built by PC(USA) mission funds. Soon joy replaced despair. The language was passionate. The hospitality was contagious. And the singing was simply transformative.

After preaching in tandem with Makei Masongo, the pastor—a call-and-response kind of proclamation where my carefully prepared notes ceased to matter—I found myself gently rocking with the rhythmic singing of the women. No organ, no piano, just the human voice reverberating with gentle intensity—a harmony that sang the sweetness of God's soul. At the end of the service I received the best compliment I received all year: "Susan, you must be part Zulu woman!"

What I discovered in South Africa is that the reverent order of Reformed worship is most effective when it is matched with reverent ardor. Across the United States we are beginning to discover worship wealth as our hearts meet our minds, as our bodies begin to feel the passion of our souls. And everywhere, it is participation—the moving as well as the hearing, the doing as well as the thinking, the responding as well as the receiving—that helps us find God in the wonder of worship.

The educators in our midst have long encouraged us to engage our multiple intelligences in our worship and learning, making sure that we are glorifying and enjoying God with our hearts, our minds, our bodies, and our souls. Reverence can meet joy, mystery can engage emotion, thinking can partner with clapping, as we live in the order/ardor paradox of the Presbyterian Way.

And the more we open up to the multicultural reality of modern America, the more we can learn from our global and ethnic partners how to experience God with all the senses and all the passions of our hearts.

2. *Providence and partnership.* At the heart of our Reformed theology is the sovereignty of our providential God. We start with God, we end with God, and we affirm that God initiates all the blessings of every day. Any attempt to put ourselves in the center—to place *our* power, *our* ambitions, *our* abilities as the focus of existence—such human *hubris* denies the gift of creation and the power of the Creator.

And yet in an astounding act of generosity, God Almighty invites us to partner with God to continue the work of creation. In the act of incarnation, the Word becoming flesh in Jesus of Nazareth, the Powerful One comes to be one with us, to be one of us, to take our creatureliness and to imbue it with the image and imagination of the Creator. Through the stunning transformation of resurrection, death becomes life. The divine becomes human, so the human can dare to touch divinity. The lavish power of Pentecost changes the church into the Resurrected Body of the Living Christ on Earth.

One of the stunning gifts of the Reformed tradition to the world of spiritual truth is our central affirmation that all human beings have a vocation—a calling—to be God's presence in the world. Through the gifts of Spirit given to us at birth, and through the empowerment and blessing of baptism, we Presbyterians understand our lives to be engaged 24/7 in ministry in service to God's world.

In a culture that is too fast, too stuffed, too complex, too selfish, it is difficult for many of us to find meaning and purpose amid the chaos. But this Reformed understanding of vocation, of partnership with our providential God, can hook the restless seekers of these contemporary times.

In January 2004, I traveled to Colombia to share solidarity with our courageous partners in the Iglesia Presbyteriana de Colombia. Not only are these brothers and sisters risking their lives to proclaim justice and dignity in that repressive, violent place. They are also offering compassion and hope and healing to the more than four million refugees displaced by misguided government policies. In one small rural village we met with the members of the new Presbyterian church—all of them peasants who had been forced off their land in the mountains. Now desperately poor, hungry, and unemployed, they were trying to start over with the help of the church. I asked one weathered old farmer why he was now a Presbyterian, rather than resuming his previous Roman Catholic faith. His answer was immediate, and very Presbyterian: "Because when we arrived in this village with nothing, the Presbyterians came out to meet us in our distress. And because in the Presbyterian Church, we all get to be leaders, to decide together how to be the body of Christ." Providence acted out through partnership in the dire poverty of Colombia!

3. *Sin and sanctification.* One of my earliest childhood memories of the church was sitting through the three-hour community Good Friday service

each year. My father was always one of the preachers proclaiming the seven last words of Christ from the cross. My mother was always a soloist, usually sharing her rich contralto voice through the anguished words of "He Was Despised" from *Messiah*. Though it was a sad and somber day, I never felt scared or judged or bored. I simply felt loved by this strong, silent Jesus who suffered not for me, but with me. My adult journey of faith has always found its starting point at the foot of that cross.

The passion of Christ rests in the reality of human sin—in our inevitable imperfection and separation from God. Though there are certainly sinful acts, the Reformed understanding of sin is rooted more in the human way of being, always restless and unfinished until we find our rest in God. I am acutely aware of the sins of my soul, my innate selfishness and tendency to judge, my impatience with the ways of God, and my intensity of *doing* at the expense of *being*. But because of those outstretched arms on the cross, experienced so viscerally as a child, I am enormously comforted by a God who endures imperfection and pain and failure with me, and forgives me and sets me free. And with that liberation and forgiveness comes the power continually to become new and transparent to the image of God within me.

Sanctification is the process of becoming holy, initiated by a living Spirit and then lived out in a life of faithfulness. It is the process of salvation, begun with God's utterly free gift of grace, but fleshed out with the disciplines of the Christian life. Even though we wake up each morning as sinners, we are redeemed each day as cherished, beloved, empowered disciples, on the way to becoming wholly reconciled to God, to one another, and to the world. Rather than being motivated by guilt, we are inspired by possibility and recreated daily by a living God, who conquers sin and death through life.

4. *Grace and truth.* All through Scripture there is the dynamic tension of a God who loves us unconditionally just the way we are, but who calls us to wholeness through righteous and faithful living. The theme of the 215th General Assembly was taken from Isaiah 56, the prophet's postexilic vision of a recreated Israel. This "house of prayer for all people" is not a temple built of stones but is, instead, the temple of the human heart, shaped by the radical and welcoming Spirit of God. In this new reality, those who were previously excluded, the "foreigners" and the "eunuchs" (Isaiah 56:6, 4), will now be welcomed, not because of biology or purity, but because they are faithful to their welcoming God.

This generous grace, first experienced by the Hebrew people, is fully embodied in the life, death, and resurrection of Jesus Christ, God-in-flesh, who welcomed the outcast, who gave priority to the weak and the poor and small, who sometimes broke the law in order to fulfill the law, putting the well-being of people before the practices and protocol of piety. This pure, unmerited grace is the very heart of our Christian faith. Throughout the history of the Christian church we have resisted this radical call to hospitality that we, as the Resurrected Body of the Living Christ on Earth, are called to follow.

Lest we get carried away by this big-hearted vision, we need to take seriously the counterpoint of the gospel. To be a Christian means to be very specific and very particular in our understanding of this universal and spacious Christ, the Word become flesh, a Word that is full of grace and truth.

As Isaiah makes clear, some of us weigh far too heavily in the direction of truth as defined by law and tradition. But as the excesses of our secular culture clearly show, others of us weigh far too heavily in the direction of grace. In an effort to be open-minded and openhearted, in our passion to be inclusive and welcoming, we have made God's grace cheap.

So, rather than becoming an alternative community embodying an alternative vision, we have become a rubber stamp for the confused and chaotic world around us.

Now we can, and we must, authentically argue about whether homosexuality is a sin, or an acceptable variation of sexual expression. But we must never argue about the absolute necessity of fidelity and monogamy and covenant faithfulness in all our relationships before God. We can authentically argue about how much of Scripture is fact and how much is poetic metaphor. But we must never argue about the ultimate authority of Scripture in our lives. We can authentically argue about whether compassionate conservatism or egalitarian liberalism best embodies the ethic of Jesus. But we must never argue about *shalom* and justice as the vision of God's reign that rests at the heart of our faith. We can authentically argue about whether Jesus is the only way to salvation. But we must never argue about the central claim that for those of us who do confess Jesus as Lord, he is the only Way, the only Truth, the only Life that orders our living. For Reformed Christians, exclusive loyalty to Jesus is the central claim upon our lives.

Implications for Ministry

The uniqueness of the Presbyterian Way winding through a broken world suggests three implications for our future as a denomination. As we struggle to witness effectively amid the paradoxical reality of this world, our concept of ministry, our concept of mission, and our concept of evangelism must change.

1. *Ministry.* As a pilgrim people seeking to find God, we are all in ministry together. Ministry is not a profession, but a way of life. If we are all part of the wholeness we seek, then each of us serves, each of us ministers to the needs of the other. All baptized Christians are called to be the provisional sign

of God's reign in the world. All baptized Christians are called to bring about the intersection of the sacred and the secular in the dailyness of the world. The work of the Rev. Edward White of the Alban Institute and others, which focuses on the ministry of the whole people of God, needs to take center stage in all the parishes we serve. The wholeness we strive to find in our religious communities means nothing if we don't carry that vision and reality into the factories and corporations, the schools and kitchens of our living. The purpose of the church is not to ensure the survival of a religious institution, but to ensure the survival of God's good creation. Naming gifts, empowering faithfulness, clarifying values, and commissioning people to be ministers in the workplace—that is what the church is called to do.

2. *Mission*. A broader concept of ministry leads to a broader understanding of mission. If all baptized Christians are ministers, then all baptized Christians are missionaries: those who are sent to preach and to live and to become the good news in all the corners of the world. In the corridors of government and the courtrooms of law, in the typing pools of offices and the classrooms of schools, in the locker rooms of country clubs and the boardrooms of banks, in the rocking chairs of nurseries and the laboratories of universities, in the agony of soup kitchens and the chaos of day-care centers—the mission of the church is to incarnate the love of God.

Mission must not be imprisoned within the parochial walls of our church buildings, nor can it be relegated to far-flung fields in foreign places. Mission is not money or vision or clever videos. Mission is the commitment of the heart to be sent out as God's ambassadors in the world, receiving as much as we give, providing good news in gracious and global ways.

3. *Evangelism*. Finally, a church that is wandering creatively in the wilderness of the contemporary world—a church that is full of intellectually curious missionaries seeking to find God and to show God to a badly broken world—is called to do evangelism in a new way. We are not called to make everybody see Jesus. Rather, we are called to see Jesus in everybody. We are called to recognize the image of God in every Buddhist and Muslim and atheist and secular humanist we meet and to discover the truth of God that they have to offer.

Then we are called to invite them to view the world through our unique Presbyterian lens, not because our truth is the whole truth, but because our truth added to their truth may lead us closer to the wholeness we all seek.

In the congregation I serve, World Communion Sunday has become one of the most festive Sundays of the year. It is a day when we stretch the boundaries of our traditional worship and allow ardor to shape the order of our liturgy. Our normally staid choir members remove their robes, donning colorful stoles woven from global fabrics. With awkward courage they gently dance down the aisle, singing an African Communion mass. This year the words of institution were offered in five languages: Tamil, Japanese, Lugisu, German, and French. The Scripture was an Aboriginal version of the Good Samaritan. The color-draped Communion table was piled high with fresh breads from many cultures. One of the chalices was a carved gourd from Colombia.

Through confession we lifted up the brokenness of the world and the brokenness of our lives, sinners acknowledging our need of a sovereign God. But then sanctified through forgiveness, we were recreated by prophetic word for partnership in God's world, a world as wonderfully diverse as the languages and the music surrounding us.

Then, fed by the very substance of God, we were strengthened to reenter the fray, offering generous grace and demanding truth through the renewed witness of our lives.

That day the "frozen chosen" in a middle-class suburban congregation began to melt, as we took the best of our tradition and expressed it with fresh spirit. After the benediction, the African drummer began a joyful beat that led to twenty minutes of spontaneous dancing in the narthex! Somehow, through Presbyterian worship restless seekers found God. For just a moment we glimpsed the full reign of God—Isaiah's vision of the messianic banquet, when all the world will be one.

My prayer is that God will continue to reform, to reshape, to recreate, and to renew the Presbyterian Church (U.S.A.), so that with transformed traditions and paradoxical praise, we can glorify God and enjoy God forever.

May it be so. Amen.

Questions for Discussion

1. The author suggests that our Christian faith is shaped by the creative tension of certain paradoxes—order and ardor, grace and truth, sin and sanctification, providence and partnership. Where are the tensions in your faith?

2. How would you define the Presbyterian Way?

3. How do you understand your "vocation"—your calling as a baptized disciple of Jesus Christ? How does your baptismal identity affect your job, your volunteer work, your family life?

Chapter 3

Incarnation: From Above and Below

Curtis A. Jones

*W*hen I was first asked to participate in the "What the Church Needs Today" project, I accepted the offer with eagerness and grateful appreciation. I have not always been willing to participate in ventures of this nature, in part, because of the ambivalence I embody as an African American member of a predominately white denomination with, at best, a questionable history on matters of race and justice. The invitation to write on issues of theology and ecclesiology from a Reformed point of view is generally reserved for Caucasian males. This sad situation is changing to accommodate a wider audience, and more and more of the previously neglected—although not always anxious to tell and reveal the thoughts of our minds and the secrets of our hearts—are coming forward to claim our right to define, to challenge, and to change the world around us and within us. That, in and of itself, is a Reformed initiative.

The Presbyterian Church (U.S.A.) needs an incarnation from above and below to free it from a perennial cycle of empty overtures and the pernicious internal squabbling that has so marred and dissipated its life and energy far too long. We are in need of courageous, prophetic leadership and not mere conflict managers who measure success by the application of parliamentary procedures of avoidance and escape. We need to decide, and soon, whether this church is large enough for diversity or too small for God.

With regard to race, Americans in general and the Presbyterian Church in particular are still in a state of denial. The American democratic experiment and the Presbyterian Church embraced religious tolerance as a core value from the beginning; but neither church nor state has truly embraced racial tolerance and racial justice as core values in practice.

The church needs to come to terms with this basic fact as it grapples with the complex interaction between the commitment to justice and the reality of racism in the culture and the church.

There are reasons why the PC(USA) is 90 percent white. Despite this historical fact and continuing reality, the twenty-first-century church must prepare white Presbyterians and white people in America for the social, racial, and cultural shifts that may relegate them to minority status in both church and culture by mid-century.

The Reformation of the Sixteenth Century

Rooted in the Protestant Reformation of the sixteenth century and anchored in the biblical covenant of a much earlier period, the Reformers sought to validate their search for truth and meaning by affirming the authority of Scripture and the sovereignty of God, and salvation by grace through Christ. As Presbyterians we have drawn heavily on the Reformed thinking and writings of John Calvin, whose contribution to the breadth and depth of contemporary Reformed and covenant theology is undeniable. His insightful arguments in defense of the gospel and his unparalleled devotion to ecclesiology—the doctrine of the church—have been and continue to be the defining character of the Presbyterian Church (U.S.A.).

Calvin and other reformers of his day and subsequent generations labored intensely to delineate what would be regarded by some as sound theological doctrine. Some of their writings have withstood the test of time, a remarkable accomplishment in light of the Reformed credo to be "reformed and always reforming."

The circumstances during the sixteenth century that gave rise to the Reformation and the subsequent breach in the body of Christ, resulting in the creation of the Protestant churches distinguished from their progenitor, the Catholic Church, underscore an essential weakness in human character. This peculiar flaw within human beings is as ancient as the disagreement between Cain and Abel and as pernicious as the division of the Davidic dynasty resulting in the northern and southern kingdoms.

When confronted with obstacles of seemingly insurmountable proportion, rather than look to the God of creation and order, religious people have often sought ungodly solutions, utilizing ungodly methods in the name of God. The papal abuses, theological misrepresentations, the sale of indulgences, and ethnic insensitivity are all very well documented. Martin Luther's ninety-five theses pinned to the door of the church at Wittenberg castle on October 31, 1517, represented a bold effort to speak truth to a recalcitrant ecclesiastical power. The unwillingness on the part of Pope Leo X to consider seriously Luther's call for theological reform and discontinuation of the sale of indulgences, which had become a substantial revenue generator for the church, eventually received growing support from an ever-widening circle of disenchanted and frustrated reformers within the church.

Theology Compromised by Money and Power

The reform controversy of the sixteenth century was primarily theological and ecclesiastical; however, it was not unrelated to money and the desire for increased capital accumulation. The love of money, greed, and the abuse of power have distorted relationships within and outside of the church for centuries. The abuses that nations, individuals, and the Christian church have committed to acquire wealth and to sustain power are a sad and depressing saga in the annals of church history.

This blind allegiance to power has often compromised theological principles and contributed to divided loyalties, shown in the behavior of some of the most exalted church leaders. Guided less by biblical inspiration than by greed, the princes of the Holy Roman Empire and Protestant church leaders demonstrated a peculiar propensity for power that often resulted in corrupt enterprises and unholy alliances. The powerful few presiding over vast capital formations, while most members of the church had no option but to exist at subsistence level, characterized the uneven distribution of wealth during the medieval and mercantile periods.

The clerical vows of poverty and the example of Jesus had little real effect on numerous religious leaders installed to be the guardians and custodians of church bureaucracy. And never were these compromised theological principles and divided loyalties more evident than during the time of the African slave trade.

The Church and the Slave Trade

There is absolutely no justification for the church's participation in and silence during the African slave trade. It continues to be the unresolved blemish on the soul of a nation and a church still in denial. Interestingly, the conquest and displacement of First Nations (that is, Native Americans), the disenfranchisement of Latinos, the introduction of chattel slavery into the Americas, and the Protestant Reformation emerged over a 200-year time period. Christopher Columbus came to the Americas in 1492. The Reformation began to unfold around 1517. Disturbances between Native Americans and settlers were reported as early as the 1500s. And African slaves arrived in Jamestown, Virginia, in 1619.

In each of the above instances of imperial aggression resulting in death, violence, and deception, the church of Jesus Christ was used to sanction and to bless European and, later, American aggressors. Believing that they were modern-day Hebrews marching into the American promised land, white people and the churches they brought with them boldly charged forward to be the manifestation of a new destiny. The theology underlying the Reformation, the greatest biblical and spiritual revival of its era, was also used to usher in and coincided with the unprecedented slaughter of the innocent and the dethronement of indigenous nations around the world.

Persecuted elements of the European Christian church came to North America in search of religious freedom and prosperity. Familiar with what it meant to be marginalized and ostracized, they believed that it would be possible, if given a fresh opportunity, to establish colonies of hope with religious and political freedom. However, the American religious experiment, as well as the secular experiment of democracy, was less receptive to the indigenous people. Efforts to evangelize and to coexist peacefully with the indigenous people of the Americas were soon overridden by the need for cheap labor.

The settlers' dreams of utopian communities evaporated as the harsh reality of life in the New World revealed the deficiencies of their human resources. Earlier utilization of white indentured slaves and Native Americans proved not to be an acceptable option in regard to the growing need for labor. The prospect of Africans being brought to America to replenish labor resources would prove to be an irresistible opportunity for the fledgling colonial landed gentry desiring a fast-track economic solution. Human bondage—black human bondage—became the pseudopsychological compromise for a nation and a church blinded by the divided loyalties exacerbated by greed, evil, and the imperatives of injustice.

Whether this reality is an accident of nature or a sinister human construct by misguided people, its effect on the course of human history was not inconsequential. The Christian church has advocated for and benefited from the African slave trade in the Americas, the conquest of First Nation American people, and the subjugation of Mexico. While the Reformers were arguing soteriological issues of grace and atonement for white European people, the marriage of convenience between the church and state blessed and sanctioned an imperialistic policy of foreign aggression, in America. The church has still not come to terms with or sufficiently repented for slavery or the resultant entitlements and white skin privilege that have become institutionalized and hardwired into the consciousness of white people.

Widespread Denial of Racism

Many well-intended white Presbyterians wish to forget the subject matter of slavery and the implications associated with racism and white skin privilege.

And many black people have become so traumatized by the lingering effects of a postslavery era that they seldom express their true feelings in the presence of white people.

When vocal blacks assertively raise the issue of racism, they are often accused of whining or "playing the race card." However, such a description is seldom applied to Jewish people when they discuss the Holocaust and anti-Semitism. Jewish people have lobbied successfully to keep their history of suffering and oppression before the world. It is still easier for many American white people to acknowledge the evil of Nazism than to acknowledge their complicity with racism. Many white Presbyterians find it less threatening to establish and to build relationships with Africans whose worldview is more focused on issues of class than race, than with African Americans unwilling to gloss over race.

As W. E. B. DuBois reminded us a century ago, the central issue before the nation is what he termed the "color line." It remains the line in the sand and in our hearts—the great American divide. Reconciliation will not be possible unless there is an incarnational anointing of the Holy Spirit from above and atonement from below. This movement of love and reconciliation between the sons and daughters of former slaves and the sons and daughters of former slaveholders will require death and resurrection and struggle. The struggle for truth is painful.

Crisis of Leadership

This predicament of selective engagement and collective denial reflective of both white and black Presbyterians is a major factor in the lack of a greater African American presence in the denomination. We have yet to see that our sanctuaries are the houses that love built or that our rhetoric is matched by the passions of our deeds. The incarnation of the Holy Spirit at Pentecost remains a distant and historical manifestation, still waiting to shape the character of our church and the content of our witness. As members of a predominately white denomination, African American Presbyterians have a unique responsibility in changing the character of this ecclesiastical body.

For too long, many black Presbyterians have abrogated their responsibility to serve and to lead within this church. We are absent and unaccounted for in key leadership positions at every level, and thus have allowed and continue to allow white people to be our voice or to minimize or even totally ignore matters of justice that might well have benefited from our participation. Some of this underrepresentation can be attributed to racism.

There is no excuse for our silence and noncommitment on critical issues such as the war in Iraq; the pandemic of AIDS on the African continent and among blacks in the United States; blacks on death row; and increasing incarceration rates, unemployment, substandard education, teenage pregnancy, inaccessibility of affordable health care, and poverty among American blacks. I deplore white racism, but I also deplore black excuse-ism. Black Presbyterians cannot blame everything that is wrong in their churches on racism and white people.

We do not need permission to speak, to lead, and to act on these and other matters that intensify the oppressive dimension of life in America. Justice is not a matter in which we can exercise any right of selective engagement.

The crisis of black leadership, which limits the creative potential of both the pastors and the lay people in the Presbyterian Church, often takes the form of confusion between leadership and authority. Authority can be given or delegated, while leadership must be earned. Authority seeks permission, while leadership seeks opportunity. One cannot be appointed a leader. The people being led must confer leadership. True leadership cannot be attributed to the title or the inherent function of the pastor. Not everyone with the prefix "Reverend" affixed to his or her name is a leader.

Needed: A Prophetic Black Witness

It is time for black Presbyterians to look deep into their souls in search of a voice and prophetic standing. What role and contribution do we bring to the table? And of equal if not greater importance, what role and relationship will black Presbyterians have with the rest of the African American community?

The socioeconomic status of black Presbyterians tends to be middle income and middle class. Much of the black Presbyterian membership has benefited from the gains of the civil rights movement, affirmative action, greater access to housing and educational opportunities, and related changes for the better. However, many black Presbyterians who were alive during the civil rights movement did not march or protest with those brave pioneers for freedom and justice. They have reaped many of the benefits, but they did not bear the cross or pay the price of freedom with their blood.

Black Presbyterians who sat out the civil rights movement are indebted to numerous people—particularly in the non-Presbyterian black churches—who marched, sang, bled, and died their way into a new reality. Black Presbyterians should hear afresh Jesus' words, "From everyone to whom much has been given, much will be required" (Luke 12:48).

It is fair to say that minimal integration made black Presbyterians and black Episcopalians less independent and less aggressively black-oriented than blacks in the African Methodist and the Baptist churches. Most black Presbyterian and Episcopal pastors depended to some extent upon the white denomination for their salaries, which were always below standard. Such discriminatory arrangements rarely fostered self-determination and divergence from the norms and desires of the parent institution.

There were many black Presbyterians involved in the civil rights movement; however, black Presbyterians are not generally noted for being in the vanguard of the movement for justice. And we continue to carry this distinction and perception in the eyes of the black community, which views us as reaping the harvest of the movement but not having participated in the sowing.

In many urban areas, black Presbyterian sanctuaries are not situated in socioeconomic communities that correspond to the class status of the congregations, nor do the members reside in the communities where the sanctuaries are located. An unintended consequence of upward mobility is that it afforded many African American Presbyterians the opportunity to relocate—as pioneers—in some previously segregated white communities. Leaving behind beloved communities and sanctuaries altered the delicate balance of social composition and deprived these abandoned neighborhoods of the rich reservoir of role models unique to segregated life.

During the era of Jim Crow, segregated black communities contained the African American doctors, preachers, lawyers, teachers, and business owners. As the laws of discrimination began to weaken under the weight and momentum of the civil rights movement, black professionals began to relocate, moving out of the villages of poverty and love and into the affluence and lifestyle commensurate with their aspirations and ability. Some black Presbyterians who relocated successfully maintained ties with their old neighborhood church. However, the congregation was not as successful in replacing those who left by attracting new members from the changing neighborhood, especially those from lower socioeconomic classes. Thus, the class dynamic inside the walls of the sanctuary was drastically different from that of the neighborhood.

Black membership in the Presbyterian Church must never separate us from our relationship with the mass of African Americans, especially those poor and disenfranchised blacks victimized by poverty and submerged in the trenches of despair. Upward mobility and affiliation with a predominately white denomination ought not to sever our allegiance with the least of these. The spirit of our culture, the rhythm of our being, as African Americans is the rich reservoir of creativity deep rooted in what W. E. B. DuBois called the "Souls of black folk" which birthed the blues, gyrates in the movement of our dance, seeks relief in spirituals, and is defiantly echoed in the unapologetic expression of young rappers. This is the wellspring of black creativity; it is who we are. Its origin goes back to Africa, to the Nile Valley. It shapes our worship, praise, and protest. We are still drinking from the wells of our ancestors, and we bring this as a gift to the Presbyterian Church. We don't have to forsake our soul to be accepted by white folks.

Middle Governing Bodies

Confusion exists among Presbyterian middle governing bodies relative to racial ethnic ministry and racial ethnic church growth. In an effort to reflect the inclusive church of Pentecost, presbyteries are increasingly starting multicultural and multiracial congregations, hanging their hopes on making the correct New Church Development (NCD) start-up, rather than attempting midcourse adjustments with churches in transition. Presbyteries are to be commended for these prophetic initiatives. There will remain a need, however, for monoethnic congregations for oppressed constituent groups where the environment of racism is still the prevailing reality. Effectively negotiating future trends with multiracial and multicultural congregations, while preserving therapeutic enclaves of healing through monoethnic congregations, will require presbytery administrators to be as wise as serpents and innocent as doves. Presbyteries need always to take into account that black congregations came into being because Africans were denied the opportunity to practice their indigenous religious beliefs. They were not allowed to worship with whites. When this opportunity was afforded them, they were relegated to demeaning stations during worship services, that is, the balcony, narthex, and back door. To insist now that African Americans give up their own congregations—these cherished enclaves of healing and hope—would be a gross insensitivity. Likewise, to view them (or their motives) as unbiblical, thus relegating them to second-class status, without seriously addressing the conditions of racism within the PC(USA) that were the catalyst for their creation, would be a callous error of judgment; however, it is not without precedent.

In 1983, when the former northern and southern streams of the Presbyterian Church reunited to form the PC(USA), the all-black presbyteries and synods were asked to dissolve their governing bodies and to become a part of a new consolidated branch of Zion. What remains a mystery in the hearts and minds of many African Americans is why the denomination asked black people to give up their all-black presbyteries and synods, but in the same year created nongeographical Korean presbyteries, the first being Hamni Presbytery. Even with the inherent financial and structural problems associated with these all-black governing bodies, there was a dignity within these former black governing bodies that has yet to be achieved within the PC(USA).

Caucasian people will be the new minority in America by the mid-twenty-first century. I do not mean to imply that there are negatives associated with minority status, as it has been applied historically.

We are at an interesting juncture within both the culture and the life of the Presbyterian Church (U.S.A.). The growth of the emerging majority (people of color) has added to the complexity of race in the United States. Unless this country is open to the sharing of power and the dignity of humanity, the entrenched positions of privilege from above and below may perhaps interfere again with the potential for justice.

The growth of Latinos as the largest racial ethnic constituent group poses a challenge for whites who are unwilling to address the issue of institutional racism, and it also can be a threat to blacks and other racial ethnic groups suspicious of already limited resources and a restructuring of historic entitlements. The failure to address and to resolve this emerging issue could result in a series of events that could dwarf our mistakes of the past.

Questions for Discussion

1. To what extent is racism a factor in the life and mission of the PC(USA)?
2. What should Presbyterians and the PC(USA) do to repent for the wrongs of the past, which in many ways continue into the present, and to create a fellowship in which African Americans feel welcome?
3. Should the PC(USA) start congregations that are specifically targeted to African Americans and other racial ethnic groups, or only start congregations that attempt to reach out to all people? Why or why not?

Chapter 4

Rediscovering the Reformed, Being Reformed Church

Jack Haberer

*I*n Presbyterian circles, there's a whole lot of "re-ing" going on these days. Renewing, remembering, revisiting, reconsidering, reaffirming, resuming, reestablishing, reviving, regenerating. The list goes on and on—all beginning and ending with those key tasks, being reformed and being reforming.

The "re-" prefix rolls off our tongues incessantly. For good reason. Presbyterians drive with one eye fixed upon the rearview mirror. We don't shun all innovation, but we look to our past to map out our future, and today's new ideas get measured against the great ideas that have shaped us up to the present. Accordingly, we are less likely to invent new programs than to reinvent them. We reestablish lines of authority; we do not create them. Even when exploring new models of ministry, we hearken to our roots to see if—in God's world, where "there is nothing new under the sun"—we can find precedents that instruct us on how we can really "reintroduce" an old model of ministry.

We Presbyterians also tend to think that problems and failures of service and leadership result from shunning or just forgetting whence we came. We look to our past to diagnose our problems and to prescribe our cures.

Today's church has lots of problems simply being the church. The church, in particular, the Presbyterian Church (U.S.A.), desperately needs to rediscover what it means to be the church, to have a Reformed ecclesiology—a doctrine of the church. This paper hopes to reexplore, to reconsider, rediscover, and to reaffirm the reformed and being reformed church.

As Over Against

Rediscovering a Reformed ecclesiology offers a daunting challenge, akin to the task facing European sailors five hundred years ago seeking to find land to their west. Shouting voices from other communions, as well as from our own, make this search process elusive.

31

When it comes to discussions of ecclesiology, the Orthodox, Roman Catholic, and Anglican churches collectively drown out the voices of the Reformed churches. This threefold band of hierarchical denominations comprises much more than half of all Christians worldwide. Each defines itself as the church of the apostles, and each tradition claims that its validity derives from its lineage back to the original Twelve.

The Orthodox and the Roman Catholic churches divided in 1054. Another separation occurred at the beginning of the English Reformation, when the British Anglicans broke away from the Roman Catholics. Nevertheless, all three communions claim to be connected organically to the first-century church leaders, and they assert that such a connection was constituted by God.

A set of voices shouts from the free church traditions such as the Baptists and Pentecostals. These bodies seldom wax dogmatic about their being the only true inheritors of the apostolic ordination. Such rootedness feels restrictive, inhibiting, and paralyzing, closed to the currents of the Spirit. Rather, they simply point to their exploding numbers as they build megachurches in the United States and multiply their memberships exponentially in the two-thirds world. These fellowships claim validity by pointing to the enormous response, the millions of lives touched, the remarkable stories of personal conversion, and the worldwide spread of the gospel under their trust.

A third set of voices arises within the Reformed churches, especially within the Presbyterian Church (U.S.A.). Call it the voice of polity. Presbyterian polity, as articulated in the *Book of Order*, outlines detailed directives, standards, and requirements for ordering the church's life together. Developed initially by John Calvin, Reformed church polity grows out of and seeks to implement a wonderful theology. However, as church polity becomes the focus, theological focus is often lost, especially ecclesiology, the doctrine of the church—that is, the institutional expression of the church's theology. Thus, the ecclesiology loses its reason for being. Presbyterian polity without Reformed ecclesiology degenerates into thoughtless regulations and arbitrary legalisms—forms lacking content.

Reformed ecclesiology stands over against these Roman Catholic, Orthodox, and Anglican patterns of church organization. It builds its credibility upon the content of the faith it proclaims.

What Does the Reformed Faith Proclaim?

1. *A minimal set of expectations.* The clearest biblical and Reformed affirmation is that of our darker side: the first prerequisite to joining the church is that one be a sinner—a repentant sinner, to be sure, but a sinner nevertheless. One need only look at the apostles' letters to the New Testament congregations to validate this claim.

If you can imagine a sin, the early Christians were finding a way to commit it. They rebelled against the authority of the apostles, they scorned those unlike themselves, they exploited the gospel freedoms, they sued those with whom they disagreed, they got drunk on Communion wine, and they lazily awaited the second coming.

When it comes to church leadership, the holiness churches of the Wesleyan tradition advance the expectation that godly people will attain a high measure of holiness. The Catholic and Orthodox churches claim that a special measure of sanctifying grace accompanies ordination, resulting in a class of priests who mediate between the Almighty and their flocks. "No way," says Reformed Christians. "Sinners always are we." Echoing Calvin, they confess boldly, "We all sin in thought, word, and deed daily."

Such an admission of guilt offers the positive value of demystifying the role of church leaders. It flattens the pyramid of power, authority, control, and "otherness" that attaches to leaders in other religious traditions. Church leaders' moral and ethical failures get addressed less with incredulous shock than with positive programs of rehabilitation by the tradition that hasn't pretended away their clay feet.

On the other hand, this leaves Reformed Christians with awesome questions: Who can possibly represent God? Who can responsibly proclaim God's word? Who can honorably serve the sacraments? Who can accurately discern God's will?

2. *A maximal set of attributions.* It takes more than a sinner to serve and represent God. It requires a saint. And while the apostles' letters to the churches excoriated the sinful behavior of those there, they addressed the members not as sinners but as saints. The Greek word *hagioi*, meaning "saints," "sanctified ones," or "holy ones," attributed to the believers an exalted status. That status was not an earned one, and it often lacked visible and measurable evidence to support it, but the status was declared true because of the work of God's grace. As a preacher once put it, "Saints are not extraordinary dead people but forgiven living people."

Reformed Christians lay hold of Scripture's declarations regarding the redeemed—all the redeemed. Unlike the two-tier, clergy-laity system promoted in most other traditions, the Reformed churches affirm that all believers are sinners-called-saints, each standing on the same, level ground as the rest.

The status of justification (being reconciled to God through faith in Christ) drives a person toward sanctification—the empowering presence of the Holy Spirit that fuels an inner yearning to be like Christ. Both justification and sanctification are free gifts of God. What's more, that empowerment gets tangible as the Spirit distributes spiritual gifts to all believers for the common good, for the building up of others, and for the extension of the Christian mission. This distribution empowers every person with some form of giftedness, some abilities that can be utilized for the advance of God's work in the world. In other words, every believer is called and empowered to give leadership in the church.

Ecclesiology was not exactly what Isaiah had in mind when penning the words, "Every valley shall be lifted up, and every mountain and hill be made low" (40:4). Nevertheless, the Reformed church does follow the lead of New Testament Scriptures by bringing all its members to the same level. Leaders humbly acknowledge that they are sinners as are the rest. All members, novices included, are justified together. All are filled with the Holy Spirit together, all are welcomed into the body of Christ together, all are empowered for service together, all are put on the same path of discipleship together, and as saints march alongside one another, all are commissioned to be Christ's witnesses through all the earth.

3. *The ultimate intention.* Put together this minimal set of expectations and maximal set of attributions (as stated above, "sinners-called-saints"), and we run headlong into the ultimate dilemma of the church: How can we be the church together? How can we put forth our best efforts and make right judgments in matters of theology, worship, practice, and ordering our life together?

We must begin by acknowledging that such efforts do matter. Indeed, the church matters to God.

From the original call to Abram and Sarai to leave their people and to go to the land God would show them (Genesis 12:1), God has been on a mission that can be summarized simply as, "*You shall be my people, and I shall be your God.*" The promise to grant this elderly couple a child whose descendants would number as the stars of the sky began to unfold God's greater intention: that this people would be God's own special people.

This program unfolds through the generations that follow, coming into focus in Moses' day. It is then that the covenant formula gets articulated as God's mission statement. "Say therefore to the Israelites, 'I am the LORD, and I will free you from the burdens of the Egyptians and deliver you from slavery to them. I will redeem you with an outstretched arm and with mighty acts of judgment. *I will take you as my people, and I will be your God.* You shall know that I am the LORD your God, who has freed you from the burdens of the Egyptians" (Exodus 6:6, 7, emphasis added).

This mission reflects several critical realities. First, it bespeaks intimacy. If you substitute pronouns for the nouns, you get, "You shall be mine, and I shall be yours"—the words expressed repeatedly between lovers in love.

Second, if you return from the pronouns to the nouns, the structure of the relationship is clarified: "I will be the God in this relationship, and you will be the created people." One overhears the whispers of the serpent in the garden of Eden suggesting overturning those roles, "You will be like God" (Genesis 3:4); here the roles get put back into proper perspective.

Third, the covenant formula constitutes God's partners as a collective singular. To be God's "people" requires allegiance not only to God but also to one another. Had the promise been to be "my persons," then each individual would stand on one's own with God. Had the mission statement called each of us to join "one of my peoples," then we could choose to affiliate with one group to the exclusion of others. God's mission will have none of that. "You shall be my people"—many persons constituting one company—and that means that any who would unite with God must be united to God's one people.

God's identification with "my people" becomes a dominant theme throughout Exodus, and the formula gets reaffirmed in Leviticus (26:12). It finds expression in the promises of the prophets. Jeremiah expresses it repeatedly (11:4; 24:7; 30:22; 31:1, 31, 33, 32:38)—most notably in the promise: "But this is the covenant that I will make with the house of Israel after those days, says the LORD: I will put my law within them, and I will write it on their hearts; and *I will be their God, and they shall be my people*" (31:33, emphasis added; see also Hebrews 8:10).

Ezekiel points the people to God's mission many times (Ezekiel 11:20; 14:11; 34:30; 36:28; 37:23, 27), promising a transformation of human nature to result: "I will give them one heart, and put a new spirit within them; I will remove the heart of stone from their flesh and give them a heart of flesh, so that they may follow my statutes and keep my ordinances and obey them. Then *they shall be my people, and I will be their God*" (11:19, 20, emphasis added).

Hosea's family life illustrates the horrors that attach to the loss of such a promise. "When [Hosea's wife] had weaned Lo-ruhamah, she conceived and bore a son. Then the LORD said, 'Name him Lo-ammi, for *you are not my people and I am not your God*'" (Hosea 1:8–9, emphasis added). But Hosea also conveys God's promise of restoration: "Yet the number of the people of Israel shall be like the sand of the sea, which can be neither measured nor numbered; and in the place where it was said to them, 'You are not my people,' it shall be said to them, 'Children of the living God'" (1:10).

Zechariah also reiterates God's mission statement (8:8; 13:9).

The divine intention, "*You shall be my people, and I shall be your God*," is the engine that drives the Hebrew Scriptures.

Then Jesus arrives on the scene and the mission takes on a new shape. While renewing God's relationship with the children of Abraham, Jesus tests the edges of that boundary. Luke's Gospel foresees this as he quotes the devout Simeon prophesying over the baby Jesus at the time of his circumcision. This child, Simeon says, will be both "a light for revelation to the Gentiles and for the glory to your people Israel" (Luke 2:32). A Gentile inclusion in the people of God?

In the process of launching his public ministry in his hometown synagogue, Jesus initially thrills the people by declaring that God has anointed him to bring good news and liberation to the people of Israel. He then suggests that they will reject him out of jealousy because of Jesus' doing of miracles on behalf of Gentiles, as the prophets Elijah and Elisha had done in Old Testament times. Suddenly the thrill turns to rage, and the crowd rises up to try to kill him (Luke 4:1–30).

Sure enough, while ministering among his Israelite family, Jesus gives special attention to outsiders such as the hated Samaritans. He heals the slave of a Roman centurion, declaring, "I tell you, not even in Israel have I found such faith" (Luke 7:9). He liberates a Gerasene demoniac (Luke 8:26–39) and the demon-possessed daughter of a Phoenician woman (Matthew 15:21–28). Finally, when on the cross Jesus breathes his last, it is a Roman soldier who declares, "Truly this man was God's Son!" (Mark 15:39).

After the resurrection and ascension, this expanded vision for the people of God takes wings. The language miracle of Pentecost brings into this new expression of God's people, not only Jews of the Diaspora but also Arabs (Acts 2:11). The conversion of the uncircumcised Cornelius and his cohort of Roman soldiers in Caesarea (Acts 10) unleashes the gospel from the Jewish enclave and turns it into a worldwide movement.

Sure enough, the apostles catch the vision and now pour their lives into fulfilling this broadened mission of God. Paul assures that the promises of Hosea are still operative (Romans 9:25–26), and Peter downright declares it done: "But you are a chosen race, a royal priesthood, a holy nation, *God's own people*, in order that you may proclaim the mighty acts of him who called you out of darkness into his marvelous light. Once you were not a people, but now you are *God's people*; once you had not received mercy, but now you have received mercy" (1 Peter 2:9–10, emphasis added).

Paul calls upon the Corinthian Christians to live into this new reality: "What agreement has the temple of God with idols? For we are the temple of the living God; as God said, 'I will live in them and walk among them, and *I will be their God, and they shall be my people*'" (2 Corinthians 6:16, emphasis added).

John's Revelation, speaking of the ultimate fulfillment of God's mission in history, summarizes the results, using the language of the covenant formula: "Then I saw a new Heaven and a new Earth, . . . And I heard a loud voice from the throne saying, 'Now the dwelling of God is with men, and he will live with them. *They will be his people, and God himself will be with them and be their God*" (Revelation 21:1–3 NIV, emphasis added).

Why do I recite all these references? To make the point: being the people of God matters to God. Indeed, it is the divine project in the world. It is the reason why we find, on almost every page in the New Testament, narratives testifying about the formation of and/or directives guiding the implementation of God's plans for God's people.

Sadly, then and now, the people of God keep missing the point of it all. Sadly, we pour our attention into secondary tasks while God strives to drive us to our primary tasks. And we find ourselves all the more wondering, "How can we be the church together? How can we responsibly proclaim God's word? How can we mediate and negotiate our differences?"

How can we?

Getting There

Time for some "re-ing"!

1. We must *reaffirm* loudly the wondrous words of the gospel message. Good news: most Presbyterians believe that gospel. Bad news: many Presbyterians muffle its proclamation. Worse news: some Presbyterians seem to have forgotten the point and/or plan of the gospel.

What is that gospel? It is the formula that morphs minimal expectations into maximal attributions. It is the solution that turns sinners into saints. It is the mechanism by which some people of the world become people of God.

So what is the gospel? It is the good news that out of an incomprehensible love, God gave God's only begotten Son, that whosoever believes on him should not perish but have eternal life. What is the intent of the gospel? To forgive, reconcile, restore, redeem, and bring a multitude of humans into relationship with God. What is the method of the gospel? The reconciling work of the incarnate Son, Jesus, who died for the sins of the world, and who rose triumphant from the dead, thereby freeing all believers from the power of death. How does that gospel get realized? The Holy Spirit, sent by God, inspires the proclamation of the gospel in the world, extends the gift of grace to countless numbers of persons, draws those persons through the waters of baptism, and woos many to turn from their rebellion against God to place their trust in that gospel to save them.

This good news message gets expressed implicitly in the liturgies of the Reformed churches. This message is preached explicitly in many of our pulpits. But too many pastors have assumed mistakenly that their members all get it. In the process, familiarity has bred complacency.

At the risk of sounding trite, to rediscover itself, the church must make the main thing the main thing. The gospel is the main thing. It is the core proclamation of the church. Note the operative term: proclamation. Too quickly we move from proclamation to exhortation, from declaring good news to promoting good behavior, from celebrating to cajoling. Obviously, it is appropriate to impress upon one another the need to serve, to maintain good morals, to reach out. Jesus taught us to do so, and the apostles echo such urgings. But they promoted such actions as the outgrowth of gratitude, the gratitude that comes from the realization that the good news is such an amazing grace.

If the church is going to rediscover its Reformed center, it must outshout the television advertisements, letting the world know that Jesus' life, ministry, death, resurrection, ascension, and gift of the Holy Spirit make all the difference in the world, and that by that work of Christ, "all things are become new."

The message of the gospel must be proclaimed undiluted and unmuted. It must be affirmed as nonnegotiable and unequivocal.

2. We must *reengage* God's worldwide, cross-cultural mission. The model established on the Mount of Olives just before Jesus' ascension is telling. "But you will receive power when the Holy Spirit has come upon you; and you will be my witnesses in Jerusalem, in all Judea and Samaria, and to the ends of the earth" (Acts 1:8). Biblical scholars generally see that movement as the driving outline of the narrative of the Acts of the Apostles. Missiologists generally see that movement as the driving paradigm for the acts of the vital contemporary church, indeed, a four-layered program for the mission work of God's people.

What is the four-layered paradigm for mission? Layer 1: reaching one's own people group, the "Jerusalem" of our local environment. Layer 2: reaching the larger population around us, the "Judea" of our region. Layer 3: reaching those nearby but in different culture groups, the "Samaria" of folks unlike us. Layer 4: reaching all peoples in all the world, the "ends of the earth" with all their different languages and cultures.

At its best the church has broken out of its familiar walls and has relinquished its traditional patterns of work and worship in order to convey the gospel of Christ across cultural and geographical divides. Too often, though, the church has tried to export an enculturated form of its religion, thereby dissipating its effectiveness and trampling upon the valid structures and styles of others' traditions and cultures. Much too often, the church has just shrugged off those unlike itself.

The early Christians found themselves caught between their commitment to the tradition and their commission to make disciples of all nations. Those first Christians were, after all, the children of Abraham, Isaac, and Jacob. They had been raised according to the law of Moses. And Jesus taught that "not one letter, not one stroke of a letter, will pass from the law until all is accomplished" (Matthew 5:18). That law obviously must include the mark of the covenant, the entry point for converts, the act of circumcision. It must also include the most obvious public witness of Israel, the keeping of the Sabbath. And surely it must refuse all association with idolatry.

Then came the conversion of Cornelius and his cohort of Roman soldiers, who received the baptism of the Holy Spirit by sovereign visitation, and then were baptized by the leader of the apostles. What were the church leaders to do? They wrestled, prayed, and argued together. They concluded that circumcision could be set aside. The new entry point for faith would be baptism. In time they also concluded that Sabbath keeping was no longer binding. And eating food offered to idols—theretofore an unthinkable act—would be tolerated, just as long as doing so would not become a stumbling block, tripping up those entering into the faith community.

Then again, some folks found this Christian ethic to be so liberating that they threw off all cultural norms and forms. They took their liberties to extremes, proclaiming that the truth had set them free from old traditions. But the same Paul who diminished so many Mosaic laws excoriated the libertines for eschewing cultural norms, and challenged them to become more self-denying, lest their liberated lifestyles become stumbling blocks to tenderfoot believers.

The apostles were overcoming all barriers to spread the gospel to as many as imaginable. They refused to allow either old traditions or new eccentricities to weaken the impact of the message they proclaimed.

Today's church seems to be pulled back into traditions and forms of religion that are antiquated and even reactionary. Then again, the church is also being pulled into the promotion of liberties that offend the moral sensibilities of even the nominally ungodly. The gospel gets muted in the process.

The church needs to reengage God's worldwide, cross-cultural mission, even if that requires us to update our choice of music, our preference for familiar terms, and our control over what we can expect to happen when we are gathered or scattered. The church also needs to throw off those innovations that discredit the gospel proclamation. Sorting through all these options requires intense study and reflection. But the ultimate measure of such work is simply, Is this helping spread the gospel message to the world or not?

3. We need to *recommit* ourselves to one another. Given that God's program for the ages is building a people for God, and given the enormous emphasis placed upon the church's unity in such books as the Gospel and Epistles of John, 1 Corinthians, and Ephesians, the unity of the church matters. The post-Reformation era has been scandalized by its multiplication of denominations, and one does not foster God's purposes by drawing yet another dividing line.

While we may not undo all the divisions that have accumulated over five centuries since the Protestant Reformation, given Jesus' prayer for unity, one may generally surmise that any movement toward unity is probably a movement in the direction God would have us go, and movement toward yet another schism is probably movement contrary to where God would have us go.

In a time when independence reigns, we need to reclaim the value of denominational affiliation. The mainline churches in general and the Reformed churches in particular put their members into covenant accountability with people they would not have chosen as friends. No doubt such partnering can feel like pulling a plow in zigzag lines with unequally yoked animals. Then again, a cross-pollinating, mutual learning process, comparable to the seminar style of class work, can result for those willing to engage the varied points of view.

Like the diamond with its many facets, about half of which are always obscured from one's own eyes, we need each other to see better the sides of truth not fully comprehended, indeed (true to our sinning tendencies), the sides of truth we would rather not see.

Of course, we can gain much by dialogue with those of other Christian communities. But as in the nuclear-family experience, the learning is intensified when we know that at the end of the day, we do not retreat into separate enclaves but actually have to live together in mutual commitment, covenant, and accountability.

We need to recommit ourselves to one another, so that we may live out our Christian covenant as the growing people of God.

4. The Reformed, reforming church must *rekindle* its passion for God. "You shall be mine, and I shall be yours," say lovers in love. So says God to God's people. Just as the fires of romance tend to fade in a marriage, so the boiling waters of love for God too easily turn lukewarm. John warns the church of Laodicea that such tepid devotion will lead to being spit out of God's mouth (Revelation 3:16). We cannot abide a lukewarm engagement of our faith either. In our praying and our singing, in our times of celebration and in our times of contemplation, we must risk letting go of our safe analysis in order to follow the Shema, the great love commandment. If obedience were enough, Moses would have commanded his people "to obey the LORD your God with all your heart, and with all your soul, and with all your might." Considering Moses' role as lawgiver, that might be the command we would expect. But Moses then, and Jesus later, commanded their followers to "love" God. Can we afford to do less?

Conclusion

The church needs to do some "re-ing": reaffirming the gospel proclamation; reengaging God's worldwide, cross-cultural mission; recommitting ourselves to one another; rekindling our passion for God. None of these ideas is terribly new. Rightly so. We do need to drive with one eye fixed upon the mirror. But we do need to drive forward into God's ever-broadening mission with conviction, with passion, with vision, and with an irrepressible love for God. We do need to reexplore, to reconsider, to rediscover, and to reaffirm the ever-Reformed and ever-being-reformed church.

Questions for Discussion

1. Describe the three patterns of church government as outlined by the author. What are the benefits of the Presbyterian form of government?
2. Ask each member of the class to write down his or her definition of the "gospel." How much agreement or disagreement did you find? After hearing all, can the class agree on a single definition?
3. How important is worship, and especially music, in communicating with the unchurched in today's culture?

Chapter 5

The Reformed Theological Tradition:
A Way of Being Christian

John Buchanan

I fell in love with the Reformed tradition, and it began to be formative for me before I had a name for it. I became a Presbyterian when the local Presbyterian pastor heard that a new young couple in the neighborhood had a sick baby and he paid a visit in their home. They were so taken with his kindness and his prayers for their child that they joined his congregation and took the infant to church one Sunday for baptism.

The minister's name was the Rev. Mason Cochrane, and although I do not recall meeting him until many years later, he held me in his arms, poured the waters of baptism on my head, and assured my parents of the covenant promise of God. He told the congregation sitting in the pews that Sunday morning that they were my sponsors, my "Presbyterian God-parents." He instructed the congregation of its responsibility to nurture me in the faith so that one day I would confess Jesus Christ as my Lord and Savior and come, at the last, to his eternal kingdom.

That baptism took, as far as I'm concerned. I grew up in that congregation, and it was there that I first asked the kinds of questions that brought me to my vocation as a minister.

I loved the Reformed tradition before I had a name for it. And even though the tradition chose me, as it were, I early on started to choose it and claim it as my own.

Mason Cochrane was followed by Robert Graham, an eloquent Texan who enthralled us with his sonorous voice. On Good Friday night, at a candlelight service during which he read the accounts of the crucifixion and cried out, loudly, in the darkened sanctuary, *"Eloi, Eloi, lama sabachthani,"* I was touched to the quick with the pathos of the passion.

But it was the Rev. Leslie Van Dine who made me a Presbyterian and life-long lover of the Reformed tradition. Van Dine was a decorated Army sergeant in World War II whose call to ministry came in the intensity and mortal danger of combat. After the war he went to college and on to Yale Divinity School and then came to us. Yale! I didn't know about university divinity schools.

Van Dine had an odd voice, small and high for a big man. He pretty much read his sermons, I recall. But he was a reader, and he laced his sermons with references to books and essays and movies. He even quoted the *New York Times*! My parents were entranced. Even when his Democratic politics irritated my thoroughly Republican father, Dad still admired the pastor's intellect and courage.

In a controversial sermon, Van Dine once said he didn't hope that everyone would agree with him. He did hope that, even in disagreement, his people would respect him. My parents did, and I became aware of a unique way of being Christian, which included a thoughtful engagement with the intellectual and political life of the world outside the doors of the church.

It was an unforgettable day when Van Dine criticized the Daughters of the American Revolution, a conservative organization that included in its local chapter membership Dad's sisters, my aunts Inez and Peg. The DAR, which owned Washington's Constitution Hall, had denied Marian Anderson, an elegant and distinguished vocalist, the right to sing, because she was an African American. Van Dine publicly criticized the venerable organization and said, perhaps quoting someone else, that "the best part of the DAR was underground!" My parents, not exactly social activists, loved it. The congregation—schoolteachers, a few physicians, and bankers—was stunned.

Van Dine and the theological tradition he represented, which I now know was Presbyterian, Reformed at its very best, took the life of the mind, my mind and intellect, seriously. He persuaded the Sunday school to adopt the new Presbyterian Faith and Life curriculum, the first graded Christian education resource, and I received those wonderful hardcover books *The Master's Men*, *Fire upon the Earth*, *The Bible Speaks to You*, and even when unread, those volumes reminded me that Christian faith is not only compatible with the life of the mind; some of it could be conveyed in honest-to-goodness, academic-appearing textbooks.

Van Dine also took the world seriously. Racial prejudice was an appropriate topic for biblical, theological critique from the pulpit. He surprised his congregation, and delighted me, by getting involved in our community and city and helped organize a council of churches, I recall.

While all this was going on in my Presbyterian congregation, I was attending a large evangelical Baptist church on Sunday evening with my next-door neighbor chums. The Baptist youth group (BYPU) was a lot livelier than our small Westminster Fellowship. The music was interesting and singable, the meetings featured Bible memorization contests at which I excelled, and they had picnics, hayrides, and food at every occasion. They also paid a lot of attention to matters that didn't seem to concern Mr. Van Dine, like smoking and drinking, playing cards, dancing. I am extremely grateful to the Baptists for making me memorize Scripture and reminding me regularly that it is imperative to choose, to decide, to be a disciple. But the counterpoint between the incipient otherworldly faith of my Sunday evening chums and Van Dine's robustly this-worldly religion made me a grateful Presbyterian.

It was sitting in that Presbyterian sanctuary that I first heard J. S. Bach's "Jesu, Joy of Man's Desiring" and knew that, as Virginia Wirtz was struggling with its almost mystical counterpoint, I was hearing something important and durable. Sitting in that pew one morning, as we started to sing the opening hymn, "Joyful, Joyful We Adore Thee," Mother nudged me and pointed to the name of the composer at the top of the page—Ludwig van Beethoven.

What finally compelled me was my first experience with science, Darwin, evolution, and Genesis 1 and 2. When I told my Baptist buddies that I heard and was entertaining the notion that creation took a long time, a lot longer than seven days, and that maybe we had evolved, they went ballistic and hauled me off to talk to an authority who could prove the historic accuracy of Genesis. When I mentioned it to Mr. Van Dine, he smiled and said, "Yes, that's [evolution] generally how we believe it happened, and it is perfectly compatible with what we believe is important to know and believe about God."

Intellectual rigor, intentional worldliness, an open-minded trust in God—the Reformed tradition given to me by the community of Presbyterian Christians who promised to nurture me and to be my sponsors.

The Presbyterian Church (U.S.A.) sees itself as an institutional expression of the Reformed tradition. When we ordain and install ministers and church officers, elders and deacons, the moderator asks each candidate a list of ten questions. The first question asks each candidate to trust in Jesus Christ as "Savior, acknowledge him Lord of all and Head of the Church, and through him believe in one God, Father, Son, and Holy Spirit" (*Book of Order*, G-14.0405). The Presbyterian Church, in this first ordination question, affirms the lordship of Jesus Christ in the world and the church, and the christological nature of our theology. It is through Jesus Christ that we believe in the triune God.

The second question posits the Reformation focus on the centrality and authority of Scripture and places our trust in Scripture in the context of our historic experience that words of Scripture become God's word to the church and us, as individuals, by the work of the Holy Spirit.

In the third ordination question, the church names and claims its institutional bedrock: "Do you sincerely receive and adopt the essential tenets of the Reformed faith as expressed in the confessions of our church as authentic and reliable expositions of what Scripture leads us to believe and do, and will you be instructed and led by those confessions as you lead the people of God?"

Every time I hear that question, or ask it in the context of the liturgy for ordination, I marvel at its complexity, not to mention its length, and the powerful way it identifies the foundation of our church—"the essential tenets of the Reformed faith." Someone from outside might wonder why, if we regard the "essential tenets of the Reformed faith" as worthy of adoption, we don't identify them and ask candidates for ordination to affirm and subscribe to them.

Why, instead, do we refer the candidate to a book, the *Book of Confessions*, a rather big book at that, containing eleven separate creeds and confessions spanning the entire history of the Christian church from the earliest days, from the Nicene and Apostles' creeds, through the sixteenth-century Reformation, the explosive upheavals of the twentieth century, right up to the present, A Brief Statement of Faith—Presbyterian Church (U.S.A.) 1983–84, a big book of 370 pages, including index?

The reason why we don't list the "essential tenets of Reformed faith" is that Reformed faith—the Reformed tradition—is not a list of theological propositions. It is a tradition, a living tradition at that, and a living tradition resists being pinned down too precisely, instead preserving its own energy and responsibility to respond to history, which is constantly changing. Each of the eleven creeds and confessions in the *Book of Confessions* has a historic context. And that fact means that Presbyterians, reflecting that responsive Reformed tradition, will always be writing new statements of faith and will never be content and convinced that we finally have got it all right, that finally, once and for all, we have nailed Christian faith down tightly.

At various times in our life as a Presbyterian Church, some of us have wanted to do that, to identify and express a list of essential tenets. In the last century it happened two times in particular, each a product of some in the church believing that the Christian faith itself was under attack from hostile forces in the culture: the fundamentalist-modernist debates in the early part of the twentieth century, and the controversy surrounding the Re-imagining God Conference and related issues in the 1990s. In both instances, some believed that the historic confessions of the church did not adequately express the Reformed tradition and that the church needed to say, as precisely as possible, what the essential tenets are.

Both efforts, and others like them, failed. And the reason is that the Reformed tradition is not a list of beliefs but a way of being Christian, a way of being a church of Jesus Christ.

Professor Anna Case-Winters proposes in her essay in this volume that the Reformed motto, "*Ecclesia reformata, semper reformanda*," challenges all of us, however we define ourselves on the theological spectrum. She also observes that when we are arguing and disputing with one another in the church, a particularly and thoroughly Presbyterian habit, we try to appropriate the Reformed tradition and motto and press them into the service of our own agendas and sometimes even wield them as weapons against those who differ from us.

Presbyterian theologian Brian Gerrish offers a helpful observation regarding statements of belief, creeds, and confessions: "Their primary use is not to smoke out heresy but, through constant recollection, to preserve identity. They prevent disintegration by maintaining a common language, a community of discourse, without which the fellowship would suffer group amnesia and might dissolve in a babble of discordant voices."[1]

I think the Reformed tradition, to the degree that we twenty-first-century Presbyterians understand it and appropriate it for the realities of our time, can energize and guide us into the future. And I believe that to the degree we give up on this tradition and abandon it, we put our church in peril.

I proposed ten years ago, and believe even more deeply today, that "traditional religion," make that "Reformed traditional," "as it lives and is expressed by traditional churches, is important in ways the culture seems to understand even when we don't. Reformed faith responds creatively and positively to the questions that are being asked by our culture: questions of meaning and purpose, vocation and values, hope and fear."[2]

The Reformed tradition was given to me by a congregation of Presbyterian Christians as they lived it and as their ministers were guided by it in their vocation of preaching. It is not a list of specific beliefs but a way of being Christian.

It rests on trust in God, God's sovereignty, God's gracious and good creation, the God-given freedom and responsibility of the human creature, a realistic appraisal of the human condition, and an always hopeful trust in God's care and providence—all of it growing out of the revelation of God in Jesus Christ, who is the head of the church and Lord of all.

Cynthia Campbell, president of McCormick Theological Seminary, in her opening convocation address for the 2004 fall term told the gathered seminary community that the Reformed tradition can best be understood in terms of "practices, habits." With her permission I will use her paradigm and expand upon it from my own experience.

Critical Thinking

The first Reformed practice, or habit, is critical thinking. Because the sovereignty of God is central to the tradition, we understand that nothing else is sovereign: no earthly monarch, no institution, no creed or statement of faith. Furthermore, because of our willingness to be realistic about the human condition, our stubborn unwillingness to abandon or disguise what the Reformed tradition has said about the universality and originality of human sin, we know that all human institutions, including and particularly the church, are in need of critical thinking, criticism, and reformation.

Because of the tradition's emphasis on God's sovereignty, its adherents have always been critical of and often persecuted by political entities that are overinvested in their own sovereignty. It is no accident that the only minister to sign the Declaration of Independence was John Witherspoon, president of the College of New Jersey and a Presbyterian. And it is no accident that Presbyterians were so involved in the cause of freedom from tyranny that the war for American independence was referred to, on the floor of Parliament, as "that Presbyterian revolt."

In the church, our emphasis on the sovereignty of God has led us to express a most remarkable affirmation that church councils can make mistakes, errors. To be a Reformed Christian means to acknowledge that none of us gets it right all the time. In fact, our trust in God's sovereignty inspires us always to limit our trust in church bodies, even our own.

It also inspires us to be open to critical thinking outside the church. Reformed Christians are never afraid of intellectual inquiry and are on the side of intellectual and academic freedom. We welcome scientific and historic study in pursuit of more knowledge and understanding. Because God is sovereign, we are never afraid of new knowledge, new truth. Because we trust God's sovereignty, we have always seen our missional responsibilities in terms of education. And so Presbyterians have led the way in support of public education and college and university education in our country and throughout the world.

Intentional Worldliness

As Reformed Christians, we begin with the incarnation, God's coming into human history in the person of Jesus of Nazareth, whom we know as the Christ. Libraries have been written about the incarnation, but at the very heart of the believer's faith is the clear affirmation in the mystical prologue to the Gospel of John: "And the Word became flesh and lived among us, and we have seen his glory, glory as of a father's only son, full of grace and truth. . . . No one has ever seen God. It is God the only Son, who is close to the Father's heart, who has made him known."

Reformed faith strives to keep in tension the two foci of incarnation:

- that we know who God is by looking at Jesus;
- that Jesus, the incarnation (enfleshment) of God, was born into the world, loved and lived in the world, and died a human death in the world.

The world is where God chose to reveal Godself, the world God so loves as to send an only son for its salvation, the Fourth Gospel memorably proclaims.

Thus, Reformed faith strives to take the world as seriously as God does, strives to love the world as radically as God does in Jesus Christ, strives to live as thoroughly in the world as Jesus himself did, strives to follow him obediently into the world he loves.

The church has always been tempted to live away from the world, to draw the distinction sharply between the sacred and the profane, otherworldly and worldly. Christianity has always lived uncomfortably with the influence of Greek dualism, which keeps showing up in Christian heresies down through the centuries and concludes essentially that Christian life is to be lived out-of-this-world, that Christian sensibility is not about the world of the flesh but the world of the Spirit. The temptation has always been to disconnect faith and the world, the world of politics and economics, the real world in which people live.

It has been the particular gift of the Reformed tradition to insist that because of the incarnation, the church and individual believers live thoroughly in the world. John Calvin not only wrote some of the most important theology in history; he engaged the civic and political life of Geneva in the name of his incarnational faith.

Presbyterians are always to be found at the intersection of faith and culture, living out their faith in worldly acts of obedience and courage, kindness and compassion, justice and mercy. That commitment to the world means that Reformed churches like the Presbyterian Church (U.S.A.) will always be in a little trouble. Precisely because we take the world seriously, we find ourselves involved in issues and activities over which people disagree. In our own lifetime, those often controversial and divisive issues have included racial justice, economic justice, gender justice, peace, political and military oppression, and sexual orientation. Sometimes we all wish that our church would have fewer things to say about controversial issues. But we need the reminder that our church is intentionally worldly and thus inevitably involved in controversy, precisely because it is incarnational and takes the world absolutely seriously.

Dietrich Bonhoeffer wrote: "I thought I could acquire faith by trying to live a holy life. . . . Later I discovered and am still discovering right up to the very moment that it is only by living completely in this world that one learns to believe."[3]

And Reformed theologian Jürgen Moltmann: "If we want to live today, we must consciously will life. We must learn to love life with such a passion that we no longer become accustomed to the powers of destruction. We must overcome our own apathy and be seized by the passion for life."[4]

Grace and Gratitude

Reformed theology rests on the theology of grace. We share with the heirs of Martin Luther the Reformation rediscovery that "God proves his love for us in that while we still were sinners Christ died for us. . . . We even boast in God through our Lord Jesus Christ, through whom we have now received reconciliation" (Romans 5:8, 11).

And "we know that a person is justified not by the works of the law but through faith in Jesus Christ. And we have come to believe in Christ Jesus, so that we might be justified by faith in Christ, and not by doing the works of the law" (Galatians 2:16).

Reformed theology is a theology of grace, resting on Paul's understanding of faith and the law and salvation as God's gifts in Jesus Christ. We cannot win or earn our salvation. It is given in Jesus Christ. We cannot secure it by works of the law, by religious ritual, by following religion or church requirements. We are saved by grace. And Reformed theologians have understood and taught the critical understanding that the faithful life is not lived to make oneself worthy of God's love, but in profound gratitude for a love that one could never earn or deserve.

It is, Reformed theology understands, unconditional love, love with no strings attached. It is reflected in the story Jesus told about a father and two sons, each of whom strays from the father, the younger son by dissolute living in a far country where he squanders his father's resources, and the older son by distancing himself from the father through his own pride and obstinacy and self-righteousness. It is a wonderfully radical story of grace—of a father who runs down the road to welcome his young son home and who embraces and forgives the wayward young man even before he can speak the words of repentance he has so carefully rehearsed. Grace—and gratitude. And then the father leaves home to reclaim his eldest son, another prodigal, alienated by his own self-righteousness.

The great Reformed theologian Karl Barth said that the experience of God's grace is like that of a child on Christmas morning showered with many gifts.

And Paul Tillich once wrote that the spiritual challenge for all of us is to "accept the fact that we are accepted."[5]

Reformed Christians are, therefore, uncomfortable with religion that seems to be suggesting we must do certain things in order to win, deserve, earn, or be worthy of God's love. Grace is primary. God loves us. Our first and primary response is gratitude. Even as we confess our sin in corporate worship, Reformed Christians understand that grace comes first; like the father in the parable of the prodigal son, God extends forgiveness even before we get around to confessing. In fact, it is the miracle of God's love, God's truly amazing grace, that prompts authentic repentance.

In fact, the primacy of grace means that even our search for God, our personal faith journey, is an expression of God coming to us.

Psalm 139 promises:

> O LORD, you have searched me and known me. . . .
> You search out my path and my lying down. . . .
> If I take the wings of the morning
>   and settle at the farthest limits of the sea,
> even there your hand shall lead me,
>   And your right hand shall hold me fast.
> Psalm 139:1, 3, 9–10

And the anonymous hymn writer testifies:

> I sought the Lord, and afterward I knew
> He moved my soul to seek him, seeking me;
> It was not I that found, O Savior true;
> No, I was found of thee.
> *The Hymnbook* (1955), 402

The Future of Reformed Theology and the PC(USA)

We live precariously, in a time of great uncertainty and fear. After September 11, 2001, a consensus emerged among analysts of American culture that the world had changed in a fundamental way and that certainties upon which generations of Americans had built their lives, their politics, and their worldview were destroyed the day the World Trade Center towers fell. Suddenly we found ourselves uncertain about our role in the world among the family of nations and feeling not nearly as safe and secure as we had grown accustomed to feeling.

In a time of uncertainty and fear, a religion that is uncomplicated and simple will be attractive. The dilemma for Reformed faith is that our way of being Christian resists simplicity for simplicity's sake, in fact, sees danger in oversimplifying both needs of human beings and religion's response. Reformed faith appreciates complexity and cultivates critical thinking, poses serious questions, encourages intellectual analysis. All of which is to say that maintaining good faith with our theological tradition will not be easy. In fact, the world in which we find ourselves living requires unprecedented leadership, creativity, and rigorous critical thinking.

In the meantime, our denomination continues to lose numerical strength and its prior prominence and influence in American society. The challenge ahead is to remain faithful to our Reformed way of being Christian, while at the same time responding creatively and faithfully to the changed and changing world in which we live.

We must come to terms with the reality that we will not, in our lifetime, recover the prominence we once enjoyed when our stated clerk's picture appeared on the cover of *Time* magazine. Instead of expending our energy lamenting or fighting internally about who is to blame, we must, I believe, acknowledge our minority status and keep faith with it. God, after all, seems to prefer to work through minorities, through marginalized people. And so it may be that the Presbyterian Church's greatest and most faithful days lie ahead now.

Reformed Christians and Reformed churches are particularly gifted to address critical current issues.

1. *Globalization.* The economic and political implications of globalization are enormous. So are the theological implications. We need new constructs, methodologies, and vocabulary to talk with people of other faiths.

2. *Ecumenism.* The revolutionary and groundbreaking ecumenical structures of the mid-twentieth century, which benefited from Presbyterian leadership and support, are themselves changing. The future requires new structures that take into account not only Roman Catholicism but also the rapid growth of evangelical and Pentecostal movements throughout the world.

3. *Education.* Reformed/Presbyterian churches gave the world the gift of education—from elementary and secondary schools established throughout the American South for children of newly freed slaves to church-related colleges scattered throughout the North American continent. The solidification of public education accessible to all has fundamentally altered the environment for church-related education. Discovering a new way to be faithful in the context of higher education, a way to keep Christian faith rigorously engaged in the academic world, authentically a partner in the intellectual quest, should be receiving our very best attention.

4. *Authentic witness and mission.* In a world of sometimes violent competing faith claims, the challenge for Reformed/Presbyterian churches will be to express the unconditional love of God we have experienced in Jesus Christ

in ways he has called us to do. We are called to go into all the world, not to contend, argue, or battle other faiths, but to be "salt of the earth, light to the world." Our commission is clear, although we, like his surprised disciples, do not always see it.

> "When was it that we saw you a stranger and welcomed you, or naked and gave you clothing? And when was it that we saw you sick or in prison and visited you?" And the king will answer them, "Truly I tell you, just as you did it to one of the least of these who are members of my family, you did it to me." (Matthew 25:38–40)

Conclusion

The Reformed tradition, the Presbyterian way of being Christian, is in numerical decline in Western culture. Those of us who love the tradition and our church are concerned about our declining membership and believe that together we ought to be doing something more creative than wringing our hands and finding someone to blame. It is important to understand that precisely because we are an old tradition and our churches were established early in the nation's and each community's history, we are not always as flexible as other, newer traditions. Many of our congregations are in places where the population itself is declining, and so they cannot grow. Other Presbyterian congregations are strategically located where populations are increasing and are growing.

My hope, indeed my strong faith, is that when the Reformed/Presbyterian tradition is intentionally expressed in the life of a congregation, when the gospel is proclaimed authentically, when issues are joined intelligently, when mission in the world is graciously offered, there will be a compelling liveliness and a faithfully authentic church.

I am comforted by Canadian Douglas John Hall's reminder that the Christendom in the midst of which the Reformation happened and the Reformed tradition was born has now disappeared. We are in a new place. Free of the trappings of Christendom, Hall says, and I believe, we are free to be the church of Jesus Christ in radical new ways. (See Hall's *The End of Christendom and the Future of Christianity: Christian Mission and Modern Culture* [Harrisburg, PA: Trinity Press, 1993].)

I am also comforted by words spoken to me by my pastor, the Rev. Jay Walters, at my ordination in the same church that baptized, nurtured, and challenged me, and gave me the Reformed way of being Christian. It was during the charge to the new minister. Jay's good words I now know are for the whole church. He said: "You are not called to be successful. God calls you to be faithful."

Questions for Discussion

1. Who taught you how to be a Presbyterian and how? (i.e., Who appropriated the Reformed theological tradition to you?)
2. What "practices" continue to express the Reformed tradition in the life of your congregation?
3. In what ways is your congregation living out a Reformed sense of mission in our globalized and diverse world?

Chapter 6

According to the Word of God

Parker T. Williamson

> In the beginning was the Word. The Word was with God and the Word
> was God.
>
> *John 1:1*

*T*hat Word is singular, a difficult reality for postmoderns to accept. Preferring
a plurality of words, our culture finds offensive the notion that one Word com-
mands preeminent authority. Rejecting the One for the many, we make our
home in a place called Babel, known by its diversity of religious affections.

The Singular Word

Regressives[1] who manage the infrastructures of Western ecclesiastical establishments fawn over Babel as if they have discovered something new. In fact,
Babel is the product of an age-old art called god-making. Humans have made
their own gods since the garden of Eden, the golden calf, and the idols that
peppered ancient Palestine. Every culture under the sun has its god-makers,
for god-making is what humans do.

When building Babel, humans begin where humans must always begin—
on the ground. Our problem is that no matter how elevated the edifice, it never
gets us off the ground. Our thoughts about God are precisely that, *our thoughts*
about One whose thoughts are not our thoughts and whose ways are not our
ways. So we find ourselves stuck where we started, our minds enthralled by
lofty imagination, while our feet remain rooted in the dust of the earth.

Adding layer upon layer, we reach toward a heaven that we cannot touch,
until our foundations can no longer bear their burden. Then we collapse into
the dust from which we came.

During our ascent, we occasionally look from side to side, toward other mul-
tistoried structures that cover the face of the earth. Each tower is different. Each
expresses another facet of the human imagination. We know we cannot judge

one tower better than others, for preference is no measure of superiority, and in the final analysis gravity is the great leveler of us all. So we observe one another from lofty perches, assured by postmodern priests that blessedness is synonymous with diversity.

In ancient Athens, the mob reveled in diversity. Scripture describes that syndrome perfectly: "Now all the Athenians and foreigners who lived there spent their time in nothing except telling or hearing something new" (Acts 17:21). Today's Regressives describe their version of that Mars Hill cacophony as being "reformed and always reforming."

Where diversity is our preeminent value, novelty becomes our passion. To differentiate our idea from others, we push back boundaries that once defined decorum and decency. We baptize the bizarre. In Greece, temple prostitution offered a method for pursuing one's promiscuity while celebrating the sacred. In Rome, humans made sport of slaughter before the throne of Caesar. In San Francisco, same-sex exhibitionists parade their perversity on the courthouse steps, while the professionally religious call what they do holy. What's next? Pedophilia? Bestiality? And when one becomes bored with too few orifices, can the surgeon create more? Having enthroned diversity, we believe that nothing will do but something new.

The Creator's Word is singular. When that one Word speaks, creation springs to life. Regressives prefer their many words to God's One. Thus they build Babel, a short-lived celebration of syllables without substance, whose character is diversity and whose destiny is dust.

The Particular Word

The Word is not only singular; it is particular. The truth to which Scripture attests is not that this is a word about God but that it is The Word of God. There is no other. That, also, is a difficult notion for postmoderns to abide. The particular Word requires that distinctions be made between truth and falsehood. Like a laser that concentrates once-diffused light into a powerful particularity, the Word penetrates our world as "the Word [that] became flesh and dwelling among us, full of grace and truth; and we have beheld his glory, glory as of the only Son from the Father" (John 1:14). That Word in all its particularity is Jesus, son of Mary, native of Nazareth. He is the Way, the Truth, and the Life. And no one comes to the Father except by him.

This particular Jesus is a stumbling block for Regressives. In 1994, the General Assembly of the Presbyterian Church (U.S.A.) met in Wichita, Kansas, in the aftermath of a denominationally sponsored "Re-imagining God" conference. Particularly disturbing to Presbyterians in the pews had been the conferees' rejection of Jesus. Their pronounced preference was to celebrate a nefarious "divine presence" that they believed was dwelling within themselves. During a conference ritual, they paired off and blessed the "divine" inside their partners, sealing that blessing with a "milk and honey" Communion service and a litany that venerated their bodily fluids. This was apparently too much for the General Assembly of the Presbyterian Church (U.S.A.). Declaring that "theology matters," the assembly said that certain statements and practices that occurred during the Re-imagining God conference were beyond the boundaries of Christian faith.

Then the assembly turned its attention to the whistleblower, the Presbyterian Lay Committee, whose publication, *The Layman*, had provoked denominational disruption with its reports on Re-imagining God. Something must be done to rein in those who threaten the peace and unity of the church, argued Regressives, whose ideology had suffered a temporary setback in Wichita.

Thus the assembly authorized a "Special General Assembly Committee on Reconciliation" to meet with representatives of the Lay Committee. At the group's first meeting, the Lay Committee placed a Trinitarian statement of faith on the table. The statement said:

The 206th General Assembly both directed its Moderator to "establish a committee of reconciliation with the Presbyterian Lay Committee" and declared, emphatically and repeatedly, that "theology matters." In keeping with the spirit of these actions, we, the members of this reconciliation committee, affirm the following theological foundation for our shared task of reconciliation.

1. We believe in one God . . .

Who is the transcendent creator of all that exists; who exists independent of all human imagination yet who is knowable because he reveals himself to us as Father, Son and Holy Spirit—three distinct manifestations of one reality that are inseparable; who has entrusted to us as a guide for faith and life his written Word, the Bible.

2. We believe in one Lord Jesus Christ . . .

Who was, in a mystery beyond our finite human comprehension, at once fully God and fully human, God Incarnate; who was crucified, buried, and, on the third day, resurrected by the power of God; who alone is "the way, and the truth, and the life"; who declared, "No one comes to the Father except through me" (John 14:6). There is salvation in no one else.

3. We believe in the Holy Spirit . . .

Who is one with the Father and the Son; who "will guide you into all the truth; for he will not speak on his own, but will speak whatever he hears" (John 16:13); who testifies that Jesus Christ has come in the flesh; who is not to be confused with the spirits of this present age; who cannot contradict God's revelation since the Holy Spirit "is the truth" (1 John 5:6).

We believe that genuine reconciliation must be grounded in "the faith that was once for all entrusted to the saints" (Jude 1:3). For if our committee seeks to build a relationship on anything other than this theological foundation, our efforts "will be like a foolish man who built his house on sand. The rain fell, and the floods came, and the winds blew and beat against that house, and it fell—and great was its fall" (Matthew 7:26–27).

"We are prepared to sign this document as a foundation for our reconciliation discussions," said Warren Reding, chairman of the Presbyterian Lay Committee and leader of its delegation. "Will you also sign it?"

The General Assembly appointees retired to a separate room to discuss the document. Later they emerged with an announcement. No, they would not sign the document because, said the Rev. John Buchanan, spokesman for the group, "it is too confining."

What is it about this statement that you find too confining? asked Lay Committee representatives. General Assembly Moderator Robert Bohl, who had appointed himself chairman of the reconciliation effort, identified the phrase that his group found troublesome: "There is salvation in no one else."

That's straight out of Scripture, argued Lay Committee member Robert Howard, who identified definitive passages from the Bible. Two of those citations were, "I am the way, the truth and the life. No one comes to the Father except by me" (John 14:6), and "There is salvation in no one else, for there is no other name under heaven given among men by which we must be saved" (Acts 4:12).

General Assembly appointees remained resolute that they would sign no document that included such particulars. Instead, they argued that "Presbyterianism" was characterized by the affirmation of a plurality of documents, and that specifying limited truths was "un-Presbyterian." They insisted that reconciliation discussions proceed without any attempt to concur on essential tenets of Christian faith.

During the ten months that followed this initial meeting, the two groups talked past one another. Common terms were often employed, but they were given radically different meanings. General Assembly appointees argued that reconciliation could be achieved by enhancing relationships. Lay Committee representatives responded that there could be no reconciliation apart from a common commitment to the one Word of God, who is the way, the truth, and the life. It was this insistence on the particularity of God's Word, written and incarnate, that jettisoned any hope of reconciliation between the two groups.

Sola scriptura, an uncompromising commitment to the Word of God written, was a rallying cry for the Reformation, and it continues today to draw a dividing line between Reformers and Regressives. Scripture is replete with particulars. The popularity of Old Testament prophets would have soared had they been willing to mimic the generalities of their court-appointed competitors. It was their insistence on the particularity of God's Word that invited their rejection.

Similarly, Jesus of Nazareth as he is revealed in Scripture has caused problems for today's Regressives. He is just too specific, too particular, too embarrassing in his exclusivity, too demanding in the specificity of his ethic. So Regressives pull from their pantheon a "christ" of their imaginations. They substitute this christ for Jesus Christ, Son of the living God, who is of one substance with the Father, a person whom they believe was invented by the early church. In so doing, they separate the Word of God incarnate from the Word of God written, and the Holy Spirit whom Jesus promised would bear witness to his name becomes an evanescent spirit of this age, an ethereal "spirituality" that floats through the human psyche without reference to any person or any particular ethical expectation.

The christ claimed by Regressives is, by their own admission, for example, the Jesus Seminar, not the Jesus Christ whom we meet in the Gospels. The faith that they proclaim is not that which "was once and for all entrusted to the saints." J. Gresham Machen was right: the liberalism that Regressives promote is not merely a different perspective on the faith; it is a different faith.

> It is not true at all, then, that modern liberalism is based upon the authority of Jesus. It is obliged to reject a vast deal that is absolutely essential in Jesus' example and teaching—notably his consciousness of being the heavenly Messiah. The real authority, for liberalism, can only be "the Christian consciousness" or "Christian experience." But how shall the findings of the Christian consciousness be established? Surely not by a majority vote of the organized church. Such a method would obviously do away with all liberty of conscience. The only authority, then, can be individual experience; truth can only be that which "helps" the individual. Such an authority is obviously no authority at all; for individual experience is endlessly diverse, and when truth is regarded only as that which works at any particular time, it ceases to be truth. The result is an abysmal skepticism.
>
> The Christian, on the other hand, finds in the Bible the very Word of God. Let it not be said that dependence upon a book is a dead or an artificial thing. The Reformation of the sixteenth century was founded upon the authority of the Bible, yet it set the world aflame. Dependence upon a word of man would be slavish, but dependence upon God's word is life. Dark and gloomy would be the world, if we were left to our own devices, and had no blessed Word of God.[2]

An unequivocal declaration, *sola scriptura*, launched the Reformation, an event that revolutionized the sixteenth century but also transcended it. Reformation is a contemporary event, occurring whenever the Word of God is rightly preached. Where that singular, particular Word is proclaimed,

Christians experience "confession," which, as Jesus said to his disciples at Caesarea Philippi, is an act of God to which faith attests. Jesus reminded Peter that flesh and blood was not the source of his confession. "You are the Christ, Son of the living God," came from the Father, who is in heaven. This confession, the Word of God to which Peter bore faithful witness, did at Caesarea Philippi what God's Word has done wherever it is proclaimed. It brought forth life, on this occasion, the birth of Christ's church.

In this sense, it is true that the church is "reformed and always being reformed," because each time the Word of God is proclaimed, the church experiences a new birth. But in a reality that is often ignored by Regressives, the dynamic that makes the church "reformed and always being reformed" cannot be understood apart from the phrase, "according to the Word of God." Humans neither form nor reform anything. We can only testify to what we see when God speaks. Ignore that Word, and we're back to Babel.

While the future of ecclesiastical organizations like the Presbyterian Church (U.S.A.) appears increasingly bleak, there are signs of life among biblically faithful congregations within those denominational structures. The Confessing Church Movement now numbers some 1,300 Presbyterian congregations and, additionally, hundreds of thousands of Christians in United Methodist, Episcopal, and Evangelical Lutheran communions. In contrast to their denominations' inclusiveness, elected leaders of these congregations have placed in public view three essential Christian doctrines on which they say they will not compromise: (1) Jesus Christ is the singular saving Lord. There is no other. (2) Scripture is God's holy Word. It is to be obeyed. (3) God calls us to a holy life that includes, but is not limited to, lifting up the sanctity of marriage between a man and a woman.

Although the Confessing Church Movement has heretofore eschewed organization, it is very much a reality, as Christians who share a biblical worldview network with one another, share resources, engage in corporate prayer, develop leadership referral services, share their evaluations of seminaries, link publications, dispatch missionaries, and sponsor cross-denominational conference experiences.

Central in the consciousness of these congregations is a passion for the one Word of God, the very passion that sparked new life amidst the dry bones of sixteenth-century ecclesiastical structures. Measures of vitality, as indicated by average worship participation, average per capita giving, congregational mission commitments, and congregational growth indicate that confessing congregations outstrip their denominational averages by a wide margin.

Also important is the growing linkage between confessing congregations in the United States and burgeoning churches in the developing world, where there is a passion for the Lord Jesus Christ and a hunger to grow in God's Word. A freshly defined ecumenism is spreading across the two-thirds world as its churches are finding their voice and witnessing to God's truth. Church leaders in Africa, Asia, and Latin America are reassessing their connections with mainline denominations in the United States that have become tepid in their pursuit of a generic "christ." Increasingly, global Christians are welcoming alliances with confessing communions in the United States that are unequivocally committed to God's particular Word.

The Permanent Word

The Word of God is not only singular and particular; it is permanent. The motto "Reformed and always being reformed according to the Word of God" warrants careful reflection. Of first importance is its recognition of the actor in this reformation drama. No ecclesiastical reorganization, program for denominational improvement, or renewal group agenda is capable of engendering new birth.

Reformation is the province of the Creator, not the creature. Humans do not qualify as agents of reformation, for we, at best, only rearrange that which already exists. God alone makes all things new. The gates of hell will not prevail against the church, not because it is made up of humans, but because it was birthed by the Word of God.

"Reformed and always being reformed according to the Word of God" acknowledges the divine subject with its words "being reformed." This use of the passive voice affirms precisely what Peter learned at Caesarea Philippi—that reformation comes to us from beyond us.

And how does God re-form us? He does it precisely as he did when he first addressed the primeval void. God said, "Let there be light, and there was light." God brought forth creation through the proclamation of his Word.

But God did not stop speaking when he looked upon creation and called it good. He has continued to address his created order, arranging heavenly orbits and the brightness of his stars, commanding the tides, and sculpting mountain peaks. Even today, through a language we call natural law, he speaks to his universe. Toward inhabitants of Earth whom he made in his image, he speaks a highly personal Word that became flesh and dwells among us, full of grace and truth. By the power of his Spirit, this triune God speaks to and for us today. In Scripture, the Spirit brings to our remembrance the words that were spoken by the Son, and he voices on our behalf those yearnings that are hidden within our hearts, employing "sighs too deep for words" (Romans 8:26).

Because reformation is anchored in God's Word, it enjoys a particular permanence. Nothing else in our experience can claim such certainty. "A voice says, 'Cry!' And I said, 'What shall I cry?' All flesh is grass, and all its beauty is like the flower of the field. The grass withers and the flower fades, when the breath of the LORD blows upon it; surely the people is grass. The grass withers, the flower fades, but the Word of our God will stand forever" (Isaiah 40:6–8).

Therefore, those of us who yearn for reformation in our time can be confident that the Lord's promise, sealed in the person of his Son and the power of his Spirit, will be fulfilled: "So shall the Word be that goes forth from my mouth; it shall not return to me void, but shall accomplish that which I purpose, and prosper in the thing for which I sent it" (Isaiah 55:11).

Back to the Future

The Regressives' problem is not that they have gone back, but that they have not gone back far enough. Reformers, who also work from a sense of history, do not stop at Eden, miring themselves in a decaying state of human existence. Reformers return all the way to "in the beginning," where they meet the one Word of God who declares, "Behold, I make all things new!"

"Reformed and always being reformed according to the Word of God" is all about beginning at the beginning. The beginning of everything that was, is, and ever shall be is nothing less than the Word of God. Scripture speaks of that Word in this way: "All things were created by him, and without him was not made anything that was made" (John 1:3).

Reformers know that the gospel is not a religion. It is revelation. Religions—there are many—are nothing more than Babel, human attempts to reach beyond ourselves. The gospel—there is only one—announces that the God whom we could not reach has reached us. "The Word became flesh and made his dwelling among us, full of grace and truth." No Babel here. This is a house not built with human hands, eternal in the heavens, for it was created by the singular, particular, and permanent Word of God.

Questions for Discussion

1. Define the "Word of God." Do you agree with the author's discussion of the concept? If not, why not?
2. Do you believe that God's word no longer governs the PC(USA) or the lives of most members of the PC(USA)? If so, is it true in your congregation?
3. Historic Reformed "marks of the church" as set forth by John Calvin include the Word preached rightly and the sacraments properly observed. The Scots listed a third, the exercise of discipline. From what you know, how would you measure the PC(USA) as a church?

Chapter 7

A Resource for Regathering God's People

Laird J. Stuart

*O*ne of the most pressing challenges facing congregations is to create congregations that are genuinely inclusive.

A trend is challenging our capacity to be communities of faith that are welcoming and responsive to people from different circumstances and persuasions. People seem to be segregating into churches based on ideological inclinations. People seem to be looking for congregations that offer a homogeneity of belief and practice.

For years some church growth advocates have proclaimed the value of congregations being clear and direct about what they believe and of striving for consistency and uniformity of belief. This has often been interpreted as affirming homogeneity of belief and practice. In an article in the *Washington Post* Henry Brinton observed that people of like minds seemed to be gathering together in congregations. He wrote that in recent years his church, which had been a community of faith with diverse views, had "lost members left and right to more specialized, politically focused churches and communities."[1]

Even words like "inclusive" or "hospitable" have acquired divisive connotations. After my first year in seminary, I went to Seminole, Oklahoma, to work for what was then called the Board of National Missions. I was working on a Native American parish where most of the members were Choctaw or Seminole. There were two Choctaw chapels and one Seminole church. When I asked why the structure where the Seminoles gathered was called a church while the Choctaws gathered in chapels, no one seemed to know. The best guess was that the Seminoles had a building made of bricks and the Choctaws went to worship in two wood frame buildings.

I would visit these chapels and that church on Sunday afternoons and evenings. Every Sunday morning, however, I led worship in the Cheyarha Presbyterian Church of Seminole. There were usually between eight and twelve people present. There were Caucasians and Native Americans. They called themselves "inclusive." It was the first time I had heard that term associated with the church. "Inclusive" simply meant including and not rejecting people who are different. The few people who gathered in that congregation were proud of their inclusive spirit.

Such a spirit is being challenged these days.

Reformed Theology as a Resource in a Time of Controversy

For the leaders of congregations, there is a resource for shaping and renewing their vision of the church. It is close at hand, yet commonly ignored. It is what is usually called our Reformed tradition or Reformed theology.

My awareness of this tradition was shaped as I grew up in Presbyterian congregations, but it was certainly given more direction when I was in seminary. However, it was not until the recent debates and struggles in our denomination over the ordination of sexually active gay and lesbian people that my appreciation for this tradition acquired a fresh and more urgent quality.

In the crisis that developed after the *Book of Order* (G-6.106b) was amended for the purpose of prohibiting ordained service by openly gay and lesbian Presbyterians as ministers of the Word and Sacrament, elders, and deacons, a number of people responded by trying to draw together people who had different views. Jack Haberer, another contributor to this volume, and I organized several such groups. We were admittedly looking for some common ground. We were hoping people who disagreed about the ordination of active gay and lesbian people could at the very least listen to each other and learn from each other about their different points of view.

We discovered early on that people were holding highly simplistic and self-justifying stereotypes of the people who disagreed with them. Our conversations did not change many views, but they did dispel some of those stereotypes.

Seeking Common Ground

One of our groups met more than any other. It was a group of pastors called together by Jack and myself and hosted by the Theology and Worship Office of the Congregational Ministries Division. Staff director Joe Small and staff member Sheldon Sorge led our worship and our discussions. We met five times.

In our fourth meeting, we reached a moment that I still remember vividly, even though it is now several years ago. Our conversation had moved into the areas of Christology, the doctrine of the person and work of Jesus Christ, and ecclesiology, the doctrine of the church. This was a movement other people had been making as well. The initial discussions about biblical authority had led naturally into these related areas about our theology of Christ and his authority and our theology of the church and its authority.

We reached a point in that discussion where we were wondering out loud to each other whether or not we had different Christologies and different ecclesiologies. We wondered with each other whether or not the disagreement about ordaining active gay and lesbian people was a symptom of something more than simply disagreements about biblical interpretation and authority. Was it possible that disagreement was a result of more basic disagreements about the person of Christ and the nature of the church?

For a moment, a clear but chilling moment, it appeared we might have reached an insoluble impasse. I remember in that moment a sense of sadness. By this time we had discussed these matters intensely on several occasions. We had developed some bonds and ties to each other. We disagreed, clearly in some cases, but we did not view each other as enemies. Yet here was, it seemed, an unbridgeable impasse. This is, of course, what many people across the church believe today. They believe we have reached such an impasse.

Then someone pointed out that we had a resource that we all shared which might provide a foundation for continuing conversation instead of abiding division. It was our common theological heritage and tradition. It was Reformed theology. We began to realize that we were not on our own in trying to work through our Christologies or our ecclesiologies. We did not have to start from scratch. Better still, we did not have to keep going back to the now somewhat drained well of our partisan theologies. We did not have to go back to good "conservative" or "evangelical" theology. We did not have to go back to good "liberal" or "progressive" theology. We had a common heritage. We had a common resource that we had not been using very well.

"The Bear"

In William Faulkner's story "The Bear," a boy named Ike McCaslin sets out in some woods to see a bear. The bear is real but has acquired a whole mythology. It is huge. It is powerful. It has rarely been seen. The men who go hunting in those woods every year want to find this bear and get it.

As Ike enters the woods on the day he is setting out to see the bear, he begins to realize how he is impeding his own search. One by one he gives up some items he has carried with him into the woods. He puts down his gun. Then he sets aside his watch. Finally, he puts down his compass. When he has divested himself symbolically of a means of protection—his gun; his watch, a means of telling time; and his compass, a means to orienting himself—he is ready. Shortly after putting those items aside, he sees the bear.

In our conversations, we went through a similar divestiture. We had to give up our stereotypes of each other. We had to listen to each other, to respond to each other, and to develop a respectful posture toward each other. We also had to put aside our desire to win the argument. We had to reaffirm our desire to work through our conversations as brothers and sisters in Christ, not as adversaries who one way or another were going to win the church for his or her side and, by implication, to drive out the others. Finally, we had to put aside our partisan theologies. We had to get over trying to be true evangelicals or true liberals. It is sad but true that at times we all get caught up in trying to be more liberal than Christian or more evangelical than Christian.

I think that is what happened when we finally reached that point in our discussion when we wondered if we had different and irreconcilable differences in our Christologies and in our ecclesiologies.

Then, figuratively speaking, we saw the bear. We saw Reformed theology. We did not see it whole. We did not in any sense immediately comprehend all of its scope and depth. Nor did we have a shared sense of what was distinctive about it. We simply realized we had a common heritage. We had a shared fund of theology.

What has intrigued me ever since is that when the subject of Reformed theology comes up or is raised, people are somewhat puzzled or unsure of just what it is. While it is true, as several people have pointed out, that it is not some clearly defined set of doctrines, it is also true that it has characteristic beliefs and practices which when taken together make it unique.

Rogers: Ten Beliefs

Theologian Jack Rogers has written on the ten characteristic beliefs of Reformed theology listed in chapter 2 of the *Book of Order*.[2] There are two beliefs we share with all Christians: the mystery of the Trinity and the incarnation of the eternal Word of God in Jesus Christ (G-2.0300).

There are two beliefs that were formative during the Protestant Reformation: justification by grace alone, and Scripture as the final authority for salvation and the life of faith.

Then there are six beliefs that form a distinctive profile of Reformed faith: the sovereignty of God, God's election of people for salvation and service, the covenant life of the church, the faithful stewardship of God's creation, the sinfulness of human nature and our tendency to idolatry, and the call to seek justice and to live in obedience to the word of God.

Certainly our denomination has struggled over what have been called "essential tenets." One of our ordination vows asks, "Do you sincerely receive and adopt the essential tenets of the Reformed faith as expressed in the confessions of our church as authentic and reliable expositions of what Scripture leads us to believe and do, and will you be instructed and led by those confessions as you lead the people of God?"[3]

There are the so-called Five Points of Calvinism that emerged from the Reformed Synod of Dort (1618–19): total depravity, unconditional election, limited atonement, irresistible grace, and the perseverance of the saints.[4] In 1910 the General Assembly of the then-Presbyterian Church, U.S.A. identified five essential tenets: the inerrancy of the Bible, the virgin birth, substitutionary atonement, Christ's bodily resurrection, and his miracles.[5]

Such listings of essential tenets have always triggered sharp debates focusing upon the danger of subscriptionism, the tendency in the church to ignore the ambiguity and mystery of all theological efforts and to use such listings to drive people out of the fellowship of the church.

Yet for all the dangers of subscriptionism, it is nevertheless helpful to have some clarity about beliefs that are part of our history and heritage. We should be able safely to refer to characteristic beliefs.

Gerrish: Five Habits of the Reformed Tradition

Theologian Brian Gerrish has moved in another direction. He has identified what he refers to as habits of the Reformed tradition. One habit is deference to the past and the theological work and developments of the past. A second habit is a willingess to engage in critical reflection, even of what has been inherited from the past. A third habit is openness "to wisdom and insight wherever they can be found, not simply among fellow Presbyterians." A fourth habit is an emphasis on practicality: truth should lead to goodness, to good and practical actions. The fifth and last habit is being evangelical, in the sense of putting the gospel in the center of all reflection and action.[6]

Another aspect of our Reformed tradition is expressed in a variety of sources, including the Act of Toleration of 1729 and the Auburn Declaration of 1923. The Reformed tradition honors beliefs as already mentioned, but it also honors forbearance and tolerance in the interpretation of these beliefs. Our Reformed tradition does not homogenize theology or theological discussion. Rather, it has a remarkable capacity to hold different points of view together.

To point toward characteristic beliefs or characteristic habits does not exhaust the depth or breath of the Reformed tradition. But Rogers and Gerrish have given us points of entry into our tradition. They have provided intriguing subjects of conversation about a tradition that is larger than our more partisan theologies and far broader than our simplistic views of various camps.

Strengths of the Reformed Tradition

In a time of so many polarizing tendencies in our society and in our church, it should be very helpful to church leaders to renew their knowledge of and participation in our Reformed tradition. Exploring it will lead to several encouraging discoveries.

The Reformed tradition is quite literally larger and broader than so many of the points of view that get expressed in session meetings or gatherings of presbyteries, synods, or the General Assembly.

The Reformed tradition is ours. It is not something we have to beg, borrow, or steal from any other Christian group.

The Reformed tradition does not flatten or compress theological discussion or complexity, but has a capacity to permit such complexity without discarding basic beliefs and convictions.

Theologian Letty Russell has suggested that in our communities of faith we need to move toward a spirit of "hospitality and diversity."[7]

This is an alternative to the efforts at working toward unity and diversity. Hospitality places a different emphasis on the effort, a more inclusive emphasis. It also avoids the dangers of confusing unity with uniformity.

In our congregations and other gatherings of people of faith, we cannot simply resist but constructively challenge the polarizing and segregating tendencies that are so much at work among us. We can do so by drawing into our discussions about faith and life the deep and broad resources of our Reformed tradition.

Questions for Discussion

1. What are the polarizing tendencies you see in your own congregation? What are the causes you see at work?
2. Break up into small groups, and have each group answer the following questions and then compare group responses:
   What are the beliefs that are most important to us?
   What are the beliefs that are most needed in our church at this time?
   What are the habits we need to practice?

Chapter 8

The Church Is Corrigible

Jerry Andrews

*T*he church is corrigible. Thanks be to God. I say so because the vocabulary item which is its more frequently used opposite seems always to be accompanied by disappointment, as in:

"Jerry, you are incorrigible" —Mom;
"Jerry, you are incorrigible" —Homeroom teachers grades 1–8;
"Jerry, you are incorrigible" —Wife.

The corrigibility of the church is to be greeted not with disappointment—the church *must* be corrected—but with glad anticipation—the church *can* be corrected. Corrigibility is a good thing, a virtue even, a necessary virtue.

Think of your own childhood and the efforts of your parents to correct your behaviors and attitudes, to shape your character, to amend your ways, to form the habits of goodness, to reform the ill-formed habits, and generally to transform the self. Our corrigibility was the reciprocal necessary virtue to their efforts.

The church, like each of us, was not birthed in perfection or cradled without fault. She does not live without spot or mature without wrinkle. She is imperfect. Yet her purpose is to be perfect, perfectly conformed to the image of Christ. No lesser teleology is at work. The church is to grow up in all things to the full stature of Christ. So says the apostle. Our maturing is nothing less than becoming like Christ. This is the intent and effect of God's work in us. The church did not begin in perfection, prizing most her unchanging ways; rather, the church is being conformed toward that perfection. Thus she is to prize her corrigibility.

The church is corrigible. Thanks be to God.

This is not to say that the church is an unformed mass still awaiting its first formations. The church is the beloved of God and has never been abandoned. She has always been under the tutelage of God and has experienced God's correction continually. Sometimes the church has received that correction gladly, sometimes unwillingly. Sometimes we were corrected by God painfully, sometimes without our knowing. Sometimes we have known God's correction as an answer to our prayers for help; sometimes we were unaware of our error. All the time God has been correcting us. Think again of the corrective work of your parents. They were constant, vigilant even. They had a goal in mind and were not deterred from it.

Seldom have we closely approximated God's perfect purpose in us. The Scriptures teach us that we are unable to do good without God, that we are prone to wander, and to deny and to defy God's good purposes in us. We miss the mark. We go astray. We rebel. When God corrects we become more effective in our obedience, more intentional in our obedience, more willing in our obedience. We never quite hit the target, retain the path consistently, or offer our lives in complete surrender, but with God's correction we are being made more able, attentive, and active in becoming more like Christ.

There has been good correction to good effect over the years. To deny this is to declare God incompetent in all the work of the Spirit in the church for two thousand years. We have been corrected. God has been at work. God is able. Yet the correction is as yet incomplete. Our errors being so many, so tightly held, so long loved, the work of God in us and through us cannot be said yet to be complete. Further, we fall into the former patterns, forget our frequent corrections, return to earlier sins. Still, God is able. God is at work. We are being corrected. In this we have confidence: God is a better Teacher than we are students, a better Shepherd than we are lambs, a better Parent than we are children. God will, in the end, and with some good effect in our generation, produce in us and through us what was intended from the beginning—the image of Christ in us.

We have been corrected; we are being corrected. Thanks be to God.

The way this is most often expressed is "the Church Reformed and Always to Be Reformed"—*Ecclesia reformata, semper reformanda* in the Latin. So foundational is this to our self-understanding that we are called by others and enjoy referring to ourselves as the Reformed. Our manner of living and approaching life, our thought and practice, our history and current commitments, our loves and our hates, our selves, are referred to simply as Reformed. We are the Reformed. By this we mean that God has been at work among us; we have been reformed. And we mean by this that we are liable to further reformation. God is still at work among us; we are being reformed. We are the reformed and always being reformed.

Think yet again of your parents' home. Now imagine presenting yourselves to your parents, your classmates, yourself in the mirror as The Corrected and Always to Be Corrected. What could possibly move us to such self-understanding, yet alone gladly embrace it?

One thing: the purpose of our correction—to be like Christ! To be Reformed and always to be Reformed, Corrected and always to be Corrected—in short to be corrigible—is to know that God has determined ("predestined," the Scriptures teach, and we say with glad conviction) that the Spirit of God is conforming us (we not yet being perfectly formed) to nothing less than the image of God's Son. So we say we are Reformed and always to be Reformed with joy, like a lamb that knows the correction of the Shepherd leads us toward the Way, a student who knows that the correction of the Teacher leads toward the Truth, a child who knows that the correction of the Parent leads toward the Life.

Here is the pleasure in all this. A lamb, a student, a child seldom recognizes or appreciates the correction given as a benefit. Resistance, obduracy, unacknowledged limits, unwillingness to admit error, blindness to our own faults—in short, pride—characterizes us and is particularly prominent when we are being corrected. But we, by the amazing grace of an all-powerful and loving God, have attained some small measure of humility before God, and thus we have come to know God's correction as a sweet blessing. We welcome it. We rejoice in it. We say to ourselves, to the whole church, to the world: we are the Reformed, the Corrected, and the Always to Be Reformed, the Being Corrected.

The church is corrigible. Thanks be to God!

This long introduction is my first point. The continuing call to the church today to become more truly reformed, that is, conformed to the image of the Son, is to become more open to the correction of our loving God. This requires trust. The church has learned to trust ("And we know") God as sovereign ("that in all things God works"), loving ("for the good of those"), worthy of all our worship ("who love him"), by whom we are purposely called ("who have been called according to his purpose") to become like Christ ("For those God foreknew he also predestined to be conformed to the likeness of his Son") that Christ may be exalted ("that he might be the firstborn among many brothers") and we be justified and glorified in Christ ("And those he predestined, he also called; those he called, he also justified; those he justified, he also glorified" [Romans 8:28–30 NIV]).

In this brief paragraph—a brief exposition and quote of Romans 8:28–30—is the heart of the Reformed understanding of what God is doing and forms the categories of core Reformed ideas and practices. We trust:

• God is sovereign
• God is loving

- God has called us to be like Christ
- God has determined that Christ will be exalted
- God has justified us in Christ
- God will glorify us in Christ

The church that seeks to be more truly Reformed, like the Reformers, rediscovers these ideas and practices in Scripture and asks God's correction that she may be more faithful to them. This is the gospel. The church must learn to believe it more fully, repenting of her unbelief more thoroughly, trusting in God more completely.

These ideas and practices are the beat of the heart that sustains our life, but are seldom directly attended to. The heart muscle has become weak through our own failure to exercise these ideas in the ways we work out our salvation with this generation's challenges. Are those who exercise spiritual governance in your congregation able to give a competent exposition of that passage and these ideas?

- the sovereignty of God
- the love of God
- the call to become conformed to the image of Christ
- the exaltation of Christ
- the justification of the believer
- the glorification of the church
- the desired required response—trust

And the heart muscle has become weak by a poor diet of unhealthy foods. When is the last time you made an important decision—for yourself, your family, your church—that was based solely on your engagement with Scripture? That is the diet of the disciple. Christ promises to feed us with it. All else is fat.

Assuming now that the church wants to be more truly reformed, how can we know whether any call to reaffirm our thoughts and practices is a call to remain reformed or merely an instance of stubbornness, and how can we know if any proposed change is a call to become more truly reformed or a temptation to gamble away the talents entrusted to us?

The answer of the Reformed is "according to the Word of God"—*secundum verbum dei* in the Latin. This continues the motto and is my second point.

The church knows the will of God, including whether any current calls are indeed the call of the Spirit, by whether or not they are according to the Word of God. The Spirit does not act contrary to the Word of the Spirit's own inspiration and illumination. Inasmuch as Christ's will is revealed to us in Scripture, it is to be obeyed, as our *Book of Order* says. The Scriptures are the standard by which we adjudicate. The Scriptures are the instrument by which the Spirit guides our discernment. The Scriptures are the rule of our reformation. We are at our best, most truly reformed in our life, when we, mimicking the Reformers, return to the Scriptures. Whatever reaffirmation of the old or adaptations of the new we debate, the Word of God is the sole arbiter.

How then can we know, or at least know best, what the Scriptures teach? The Reformed answer: in community. The Spirit acts through the church, when women and men are gathered together with the Scriptures—open and central and having the authority of God—to discover, to debate, to discuss, and to discern the call of the Spirit.

Our pulpits are often filled with sound advice, good reasoning, well-used educations, adequate preparation, but they are not necessarily or therefore proclaiming the Word so that the church can hear a word from beyond—a distinctive and divine voice that has the potential to correct us. Our members seldom insist on it.

Current debates within the church on matters of polity, social witness, even doctrinal affirmation, make only passing reference to Scripture, and the willingness to submit together all our competing positions alone to scriptural adjudication in practice is minimal. The environments of public decision making are not conducive to sustained conversation, let alone sustained study of Scripture. Decisions are made by brief argument, not rigorous study. Reflection is rare.

Furthermore, we are seldom together at all. For the last generation or two, the stewardship of the PC(USA) and its predecessors has been given to the progressives. Many were excluded from this stewardship, chief among them the largest theological minority (there is no theological majority) in the church—the evangelicals of whom I am one. I am able to name only a few evangelicals in leadership in our denomination, now and over the last generation plus. The exclusion has been near perfect. For this and other reasons I judge the stewardship to have failed.

That's a bold and severe statement. It is also whining. Evangelicals have long become accustomed to being on the outside looking in, both complaining about the exclusion and then finding a degree of comfort in it all. It is an easy assignment to bear no responsibility for our common life and to be able to proclaim innocence of any leadership role.

The PC(USA) has not fared well lately. Forty consecutive years of membership decline would be sufficient, one would think, to prompt us to change course. A generation of complaining of the current course without any responsibility for its change has been an easy, even lazy, role for the evangelicals to play. We have played it well. We are in disagreement with every major initiative of the last generation. We are the opposition party.

And here surprisingly is some hope for our reformation, or at least the establishment of the environment for it. Evangelicals have finally organized. We have weighed in decisively on the presenting issue of our day—sexuality—and thus have announced our presence as a contestant for and in the assemblies of the church.

We now have a two-party system—progressives and evangelicals. Together they are not the whole church, not nearly, together perhaps being barely the majority; they nonetheless address and are at cross-purposes the majority of the time on a majority of the issues and initiatives before the church. In the long run this is not a good place for the church to be, but we are in a better place than we were with a one-party system exclusive of all others.

This is, of course, an evangelical spin on the events of the last decade. The progressives can now be heard whining that someone has taken the church from them and that this is not the church that they once loved. They do not, I think, hear their own self-judgment in this—that the church once was theirs, unshared, and what they loved was the uncontested leadership of the church.

Alas. We are all sinners. And here's my point in all this. Now, only now, are we perhaps ready to hear together the Word of God, because now, only now, despite the open contention, we are in the same room at the same time, contesting the same things in our common life. Contention requires contact; contact requires proximity. We are now more proximate—not more in agreement or even more agreeable—but more mutually engaged. Can we hear the Word together now? Can we respond to the call of the Spirit—together?

I am required to set before you a replacement agenda for the church for the next generation, especially after announcing my verdict that the stewardship of the last generation has failed. Though an evangelical by training, conviction, and association, some of this agenda will undoubtedly be idiosyncratic. Nonetheless, I offer it. If together we heard the Spirit call us, according to the Word, into a fuller reformation of our common life, what might it look like?

Two answers have already been suggested:

1. *Repent.* This would require unceasing repentance—repentance for abandoning earlier reformations, as if our time and place is unique and thus exempt from God's previous corrections, and repentance for being so obdurate on our current course, considering its obvious failure to strengthen the church.

2. *Restart common study of the Scriptures.* This would require obedience—the obedience of no longer arguing against the plain sense of Scripture to excuse ourselves as if it belonged to our competing sides rather than the whole church, obedience in wrestling with the corrective Word of God in the pulpit and together in discernment.

I offer three other suggestions: one each with regard to our confessional genius, our commission from Christ, and our relationship with others.

3. *Reconnect to our confessional heritage.* Reconsider whether it is wise to have a *Book of Confessions,* rather than one confessional standard. The collection of confessions now used is too easily dismissed. It gives uncertain sounds because it gives multiple sounds. This idea of a collection, rather than a single statement, as a standard is now forty years old in our 450-year-old Reformed tradition. It has not served us well. Theological literacy has declined. Theological clarity is hard to find. Theological accountability is nearly nonexistent.

Require a stricter theological subscription to our standard(s). Once upon a time, in the memory of some, ministers of the Word and Sacrament affirmed the written confessional standard and also announced "scruples" about what perplexed them or about that with which they disagreed. The presbytery then wrestled with whether or not this scruple was in regard to an essential of the faith. This practice solicited rigorous examination of self and others, honesty and integrity in public affirmation, and theological acumen.

Now, mumbling an assent to ambiguous questions, which make reference to essentials that in turn refuse to be made public, passes for theological commitment. I have been in a presbytery now for more than eighteen years and have yet to witness a theological examination before the presbytery of any minister of the Word and Sacrament entering the presbytery. If I stay to reach retirement in my current pastorate, I will have served twenty-five years within this presbytery without any theological accountability. This makes a farce of our self-image as a confessional church.

Drop minister of the Word and Sacrament as the primary reference to the office of pastor.

Let ministers be called teaching elders once again, thus reminding us all of the central calling of the shepherds of the flock—pastor/teachers.

The church has a faith. Without it she cannot live faithfully. Know it. Teach it. Require it. Tolerate nothing else, for anything else is always something less.

4. *Return to disciple making as our primary mission.* Put disciple making at the top of the congregation's priorities. Teach all members to observe all Christ has commanded—utter devotion to God and neighbor.

Put spiritual governance in the congregation of those disciples as the agenda of every session and all its ministry teams.

Put the preparation of elders in theological and spiritual formation as the top priority of every pastor.

Put the health of our congregations as the top priority whenever gathered in presbytery, synod, or General Assembly.

Put training for leaders of our congregations as the top priority for our seminaries. To teach well theological disciplines that enable a lifetime of scholarship in the pastor's study, which in turn promotes pastoral effectiveness for our congregations, is the calling of our graduate schools of theology.

Put congregational partnerships for the purpose of mutual strengthening of congregations by planting and by development at the top of our world mission initiatives. Build places that build disciples here and abroad and together.

5. *Redirect our ecumenical efforts.* Initiate sustained sincere conversations with the other Reformed denominations. There are seventeen expressions of the Reformed faith in North America, all of them more conservative than we are, all of them neglected by us. Some of them may not want to talk to us, but our invitation to conversation will sooner or later (more later than sooner, by some) be well, even if warily, received. Determine not to talk about structural church unity with anyone until we have talked about reuniting with our closest sisters of the Reformed churches.

Build closer, more missional and confessional ties to other Reformed bodies throughout the world. Recognize that together we are a General Assembly, apart we are merely synods. This will yield better decisions for our mutual mission in and witness to the whole world. It will also help us to remember that the PC(USA), still less than a quarter-century old, is in God's great scheme barely a temporary presbytery.

Bring to an end the two-generation-long lean to the left in our ecumenical associations. Turning first to other left-leaning American mainline Protestant denominations, all of which like ourselves are bleeding members, for the purpose of greater health has been foolhardy. All that can come of it is commiseration. If you put a group of sick people in the same room, you do not have health; you have a hospital ward. Instead, cultivate a closer relationship with healthy fellowships. Evangelical denominations and fellowships are growing. Determine not to sit down with Episcopalians again unless the Assemblies of God are also at the table. Purposefully seek out those from whom we can learn best practices, and engage with them in mission whenever possible. Drop conversations on unity as the first priority, in favor of common commitments to and practice of mission.

There are some severe judgments in these proposed reformations. Some of my corrections are themselves in need of correction. I do not doubt it. Nor do I doubt that the church is in need of correction, has not lately attended to this well, and has ignored the means of her correction.

Do not be deterred. Settle for nothing less. We are able to have courage in the midst of severe judgment, for we trust that God is sovereign, loving, at work conforming us to the image of Christ who will be exalted, and we will be justified and glorified in Christ.

I am more confident in God than in my proposed corrections. God has spoken in the infallible Word; my understanding of God's word is incomplete. Together we need to regain the confidence that the Scriptures read us better than we read the Scriptures, and then let the Scriptures speak to us that we hear aright and be corrected. It is the promised work of God.

The church is corrigible. Thanks be to God.

Questions for Discussion

1. How important is Scripture in the decision making of the church and the individual Christian? Is the life and mission of your congregation guided by Scripture? If so, how? Is your life guided by Scripture? Be specific.
2. Do you believe that conservatives or evangelicals have been excluded from the leadership of the PC(USA)? In the session of your church? In your presbytery, your synod, or the General Assembly? Have liberals been excluded from the same bodies?
3. Do you believe the writer's platform for reform is the path the church should follow? Which elements do you support? Which do you oppose, if any? Would you add additional planks in the platform?

Chapter 9

Reformed and Ever Reforming: Six Theses toward the Revisioning of the Church

William Stacy Johnson

Some say the church is now a house divided. Words like "apostate," "heretical," and "unfaithful" are recklessly thrown around.[1] Yet I do not accept these as God's final word on the church's condition. To be sure, mainline churches in general and PC(USA) churches in particular are marked by many differences. Yet a difference or even a disagreement is not the same thing as division.

After many years of working to heal the conflicts evident in the church's life today, I have decided that all these surface conflicts reveal a much deeper problem. Though we may find ourselves arguing over the meaning of ordination, the scope of biblical authority, or the significance of Jesus Christ, the very way in which we argue about these things reveals that we—all of us in the church—have lost a true sense of what the church is.

Our real problem is not as much theological as it is ecclesiological. The Latin word *ecclesia* means "church"; and an ecclesiology is a doctrine or teaching about the church. Running through all our conflicts is a fundamental failure to wrestle with what the church really is. To those people who argue "the church should do this" or "the church is wrong about that"—and especially to those who argue "the church should just split and start all over again" —I want to ask, "By what doctrine of the church, by what ecclesiology, are you authorized to make your claims?"

The problem is that American Christians today—all of us—operate without really having much of an ecclesiology. The American "brand" of religion tends to be highly individualistic; it has little to say about what it means to be a community, and even less about what it means to live lives that are accountable to one another before God. If we as individuals get mad at the church, then we just leave. We tend to look at the church the way we look at any other voluntary organization or civic club. Even worse, many today are treating the church more like a political party. In fact, the way the nation as a whole chooses sides between "red states" and "blue states" is almost perfectly

79

mirrored in denomination-wide discussions. Indeed, it is becoming harder and harder to distinguish the agendas of some of our ecclesiastical "affinity groups" from the ideologies that drive the extreme positions of our secular political parties.

Therefore, we need to explore what it means for us to be "church." What is it that forms our identity and mission? What is God calling us to be and to do? And what obstacles and challenges do we need to address?

With these questions in mind, I offer the following theses. They are not meant to be the last word on the subject but starting points in a conversation in which we all need to participate and contribute.

1. The church's identity is grounded in the gospel of Jesus Christ, the one who was crucified and raised from the dead. This gospel is "the power of God for salvation" (Romans 1:16).

The integrity and future of mainline Christian denominations rests in rediscovering our Christian identity, which is rooted nowhere else than in the gospel of Jesus Christ. We need to remember that Jesus' earliest followers never set out to become the "church." They *discovered* themselves to be a church without ever having planned to be the church. They discovered that they were part of a divinely initiated event. A new power claimed them, called them into being as a community, and prompted them to search out God's purposes for their lives and the life of the world. They had become witnesses to the resurrection! And if we are to be the church today, then we must get back in touch with this divinely initiated event that the apostles called "gospel."

It is not self-evident that we American Christians really know what we are saying when we invoke the term "gospel." The word "gospel"—in Greek, *euangelion*—literally means "good news." For the armies of the Roman Empire, the "*euangelion*" meant something different from what it meant for Jesus and his disciples. For the Romans, it announced one more victory on the field of battle. It was news about a worldly form of power. In contrast, when the followers of Jesus spoke of "good news," they were announcing a victory over imperial power itself. They were telling how the God of Israel—the God who once delivered the Jewish people from their bondage as slaves—was acting yet again as divine deliverer, only this time through the events of Jesus' own life and ministry. Jesus had begun his ministry issuing a direct challenge to the reign of Rome, by announcing instead the coming of the reign of God: "The time is fulfilled, and the kingdom of God has come near; repent, and believe in the good news" (Mark 1:15).

As a result of this message, the imperial power of Rome saw to it that Jesus was tortured to death. Crucifixion was a brutal, prolonged, and agonizing form of death by torture, reserved by the Romans for those who posed a special threat to their imperial rule. Usually the victims were either rebels or runaway slaves. Thus, the Romans found something about Jesus' life and ministry to be so threatening that he was executed between two *lestai* (Mark 15:27; Matthew 27:38), a word best translated not as "thieves" but as "brigands," "bandits," or "insurrectionists."[2] In short, Jesus was tortured to death next to two figures the Romans considered to be terrorists.

And yet the death of Jesus was not the end. The centerpiece of the gospel story is Jesus' resurrection from the dead. In Jewish hope, the "resurrection" was understood as an event in which all the dead would be raised up at the end of days, so that the oppressed finally would be vindicated and could see their oppressors destroyed. The good news about Jesus understood the resurrection in a way that was new and quite astonishing.

In the first place, his followers declared that in Jesus' bodily resurrection from the dead, this final, general resurrection was already breaking into the present. Through the vindication of Jesus in the present, the future vindication of the just had already begun. This Jesus who was dead was now alive to God and present in a vital, real, and continuing way with his followers.

In the second place, Jesus' resurrection was not one in which the oppressed would rise up to overthrow their oppressors, but one in which this crucified one was raised up to forgive those who had done him in.[3] His words from the cross, "Father, forgive them, for they know not what they are doing" (Luke 23:24), foreshadowed the coming of a different kind of end-time power. Resurrection was not about cosmic revenge but about divine redemption.

And so, in the third place, with Jesus' resurrection it is no longer possible to divide the world simplistically into good guys and bad guys, into "we" and "they." Why? Because the resurrection, and with it the coming of God's reign, overturns our ordinary categories of who is "in" and who is "out." As sinners, we all should be "out," and yet, through grace, God has declared us "in." "God proves his love for us in that while we still were sinners Christ died for us" (Romans 5:8), "the righteous for the unrighteous, in order to bring you to God" (1 Peter 3:18).

To speak of the gospel, then, is to invoke the inbreaking power of the one whose resurrection from the dead spells forgiveness. The gospel is much, much more than a message our preachers or church leaders can master, control, or manipulate. It is more than a set of doctrines to which we can "subscribe." The gospel is the beginning of the transformation of all things, the power of God unto salvation. And as such, it promises real deliverance from suffering, sin, and evil—a deliverance that does not belong to conservatives or liberals, to Americans or non-Americans. If it is really the gospel we are proclaiming, then we are speaking from within the new reality of Jesus' resurrection, the reality that is leading us forward into a new, emergent unheard-of redemption.

In the coming of this new reality, the church is born!

2. *The church's mission is linked to the unfolding, triune drama of God* for *the world, Christ* with *the world, and the Spirit* in *the world.*

The key task facing mainline Protestantism is to reclaim its heritage as a Spirit-led missional community.

The term "mission" has fallen on hard times. We hardly know what to make of it anymore, since what the church made of it in the past was an enterprise mixed with colonialism, hegemony, and exploitation. In recent centuries the missionaries of the church brought with them not only the gospel but also the hidden agenda of Western economic, political, and cultural power.[4] If there is to be a renewal of the missional task of the church, then we must break free from the church's cultural captivity to worldly power and rediscover God's own self-giving, triune mission in the world.[5]

When we say that God is "triune," we are not invoking theological abstractions. Instead, we are speaking concretely about God's identity. God is not some deity we happen to dream up on our own, but the one true God who is revealed to us in the person and work of Jesus Christ and is made real in our midst through the personhood and power of the Holy Spirit. The doctrine of the triune God is not asking us to believe the mathematically impossible (that one is somehow three) or the existentially trivial (that God is like steam, water, and ice), but rather something that is life-giving, something that is eminently practical.[6] It is telling us that the God of all grace has become present to us in Jesus Christ by the Spirit's power. It is pointing to an intelligible, incarnate drama that is still unfolding in our midst.

It is a drama, first, about a God who is for human beings. Before we were, God was. God created us in God's image and made covenants with us: with all people in Noah (Genesis 9:14); with the people Israel in Abraham and Sarah (Genesis 12:1–7; 17:1–9) and in Moses (e.g., Exodus 31:18; Deuteronomy 29:1); with the Muslims in Hagar and Ishmael (Genesis 16:1–15); and with all the nations in Jesus (e.g., Romans 9–11; Hebrews 7:22; 13:20–21). Because God is for us, what happens to each one of us makes a difference to God.

Second, it is a drama about a God who is with human beings. God is so much "for" us that in Jesus Christ God has determined to be "Emmanuel," God-with-us, as well (Matthew 1:23). The life that is given us in Jesus Christ is nothing less than the very life of God made real among us. The good news of the gospel is that in becoming one with us in Jesus Christ, God shows us the life that God intended us to live. Never was God more divine than in God's determination to be our God in Jesus Christ even unto humiliation and death.

Third, it is a drama about a God whose Spirit is in the world and actively at work among God's people. The God who is the Word made flesh in Jesus is also the Word made fresh in the Spirit.

This divine-human drama breaks forth in the waters of baptism and nurtures us through the sharing of the bread and cup. Baptism confers on us a new identity, child of God; a new way of living, follower of Jesus Christ; a new status, saved by grace; a new hope, redeemed of God. In the Lord's Supper we give thanks for this ongoing gift of grace (*eucharistia* = "thanksgiving"). In this meal together, we confess our sins before God. We embrace the reconciliation that is ours in Jesus Christ. We enact our unity as Christ's body. And we remember the Lord's death until he comes again, anticipating the great feast to which people shall come from north and south and east and west to be welcomed and to sit at one table with Jesus Christ as host (Luke 13:29).

This eucharistic "welcome" becomes the true paradigm of the church's mission. The table fellowship we share as Jesus' followers is meant to reflect his own practice of having table fellowship with outcasts and sinners. These gifts of sharing, acceptance, reconciliation, and welcome are an integral part of Jesus' messianic identity, and they are the revelation of God's own way with the world.

3. In the light of the church's identity and mission, we must seek a new mode of theological reflection that transcends ideology, whether of the right, the left, or the center. Instead, our way of speaking about God must be simultaneously catholic, orthodox, evangelical, and reformed.[7]

We should seek to be *catholic*. The reform of the church presupposes the catholicity of the church. Since one of the central realities of the gospel is that God has determined in Jesus Christ to be *for* us, the church must seek to embody the sort of catholicity that is open and gracious, extending to all the love of Christ. Reformation leaders such as Huldrych Zwingli, Heinrich Bullinger, and John Calvin never thought of themselves as departing from Augustine, who believed the church's catholicity consisted in it being a hospital for sinners.

What are we to make of affinity groups in the PC(USA)—whether right-wing, left-wing, or centrist—that seek to organize the church into "us" versus "them," or that invoke the gospel to erect boundaries within the church—and this, when the gospel itself was given in order to break boundaries down? After all, it was the Spirit of Christ, speaking through the apostle Paul, that told the church, "There is no longer Jew or Greek, there is no longer slave or free, there is no longer male and female; for all of you are one in Christ Jesus" (Galatians 3:28). This is the measure of true catholicity.

We should seek to be *orthodox*. Since another of the central realities of the gospel is that in Jesus Christ God has come to be *with* us, the church must seek to embody the sort of orthodoxy in which truth is relational, just as "the Word became flesh and lived among us . . . full of grace and truth" (John 1:14). In Jesus Christ, as the Council of Chalcedon (451) taught, we encounter the one who is both fully divine and fully human. God's incarnation in Jesus Christ is radically personal and not merely conceptual. The gospel is meant to be lived and not merely consigned to technical formulas. Is our allegiance to a set of concepts, or is it to Christ himself? I believe the church should return to the theological traditions it has inherited, especially those embodied in the Nicene and Apostles' Creeds, the ecumenical councils of the early church, and the confessional witness contained in the *Book of Confessions*, but it should not do so in order to enshrine these traditions in sacrosanct conceptual formulas. Instead it should draw upon them as tools to discern what the gospel is calling us to be and do in this new age. There is no orthodoxy but the life of Christ himself, made real in the lives of those who follow him.

We should seek to be *evangelical*. In response to the God who is *for* and *with* human beings in Jesus Christ, and at work *among* us by the power of the Spirit, the church must seek to be truly evangelical. Under the Spirit's direction, to be "evangelical" is to be shaped and formed by the unfolding gospel drama of the life, death, and resurrection of Jesus Christ. It is to be shaped by the *euangelion* of Jesus Christ (see commentary on thesis 1 above). What does it mean for us as American Christians to have our lives shaped by the *euangelion* of Jesus today? This question calls for special comment.

Since September 11, 2001, the American government has become intent on prosecuting a so-called war on terror. In the name of keeping America safe, the unjustified murder of 2,752 Americans has been used to justify tens of thousands of deaths, by some counts well over a hundred thousand deaths, of non-Americans. In what moral category are we to place these tens of thousands of deaths?

American Christians differ on what to make of this war effort. I began writing this article on April 28, 2005—the anniversary of the revelations of the abuse and torture at Abu Ghraib prison in Iraq.[8] I also write just weeks after the U.S. practice of "extraordinary rendition" gained widespread verification in major newspapers. Extraordinary rendition was a secret program, carried out by the Central Intelligence Agency under broad authority from the White House, to transfer suspected terrorists to foreign countries for forms of interrogation that included physical torture.[9] How do we explain the resort to torture, when expert interrogators have long known it does not work?[10] Or how do we explain our resort to war in Iraq, when we have left our ports, our nuclear and electrical plants, and other vital areas of our "homeland security" unattended? It is almost as if we prefer violence to other options.

These anomalies pose an inescapable question to the church. What does it mean for American followers of Jesus of Nazareth—that one who was tortured to death between two terrorists (see thesis 1)—to be "evangelical" today? We claim to follow the teachings of the New Testament, and yet the teaching of Jesus is clear and unambiguous in its witness against violence (see Matthew 5–7). What are we to make of that fact? Even Christians who follow "just war" principles and consider war to be sometimes the lesser of the evils must ask why the official religious text for America's response to terrorism was "The Battle Hymn of the Republic," and not that great teaching of Jesus himself, "Love your enemies and pray for those who persecute you" (Matthew 5:44).[11]

I am not denying that war may sometimes be necessary or that government has an obligation to protect its people from harm.[12] The question is how? And by what means?[13] What does it profit a person—or a nation—to save one's life if in the process one loses one's soul (cf. Mark 8:35–36; Matthew 16:25–26; Luke 9:23–25; 12:16–21)?

One listens in vain for guidance on these questions from self-styled "evangelical" leaders.[14] On March 6, 2005, after months of rumors, "extraordinary rendition" was the lead story on the front page of the Sunday *New York Times*.[15] In vain I searched news reports and popular Web sites for any Christian theological reflection about these revelations.[16] In this silence on the part of the churches, what my colleague Professor Darrell Guder calls the "cultural captivity of the church" could not be more in evidence.

Let me be clear: I want to be and I believe the church is called to be evangelical. Yet being evangelical means adhering to what the gospel demands and not to an ideology drawn from elsewhere. In short, being "evangelical" is broader and deeper than what most people in America understand it to mean.

We should seek to be *reformed and reforming*. The God who in Jesus Christ is for us, with us, and among us, by the Spirit's power, is also a sovereign God who dwells *beyond* us.[17] Therefore, our ways of bearing witness to God are always in need of reform. We seek to be a church reformed and always being reformed in accordance with the Word of God (*ecclesia reformata, semper reformanda, secundum verbum Dei*). This Word of God to whom we conform our life is Jesus Christ himself (John 1:14; Hebrews 4:12), who gave himself for us and whose life is the dynamic power that makes the church what it is. Simply to equate the Word with the text of Scripture, as some are prone to do, fails to follow what the Scriptures themselves make clear: that, first, the Word of God *revealed* is Jesus Christ himself (John 1:14); to whom, second, the Scriptures bear unique, authoritative, and authentic witness as Word of God *written* (2 Timothy 3:16); and, third, that in the power of the Spirit, the Word written and revealed comes alive in our midst through the Word of God *proclaimed*.[18]

In short, the Word of God, to whom the church conforms and by whom it continues to be reformed, is Jesus Christ.

4. The church is a community gathered as the people of God, identified with the body of Christ, and knit together as the fellowship of the Holy Spirit.

These three metaphors give focus to the church's life, but each also points us to something God is doing beyond the church's life.

First, the church—and each individual congregation—is gathered to be a part of *the people of God*. I say "part," because the biblical concept of the "people of God" includes the church but is also broader than the church. It includes the people Israel, with whom God has made an unbreakable covenant (Romans 11:29). It also includes many people drawn by God from among the "nations" (i.e., the "Gentiles"), whom God has engrafted into the covenant by an act of divine mercy (Romans 11:17–36). Biblical figures such as Job and Ruth were loved by God even though they were outside the official religious community. Hence, the sphere of God's reign is larger than the church, but the role of the church is indispensable to God's plan.

As Karl Barth put it, the church is called to be a "provisional representation" or model of what God intends for all people. Jesus said, "Let your light shine before others, so that they may see your good works and give glory to your Father in heaven" (Matthew 5:16). As God's people, we care for the life of the church, but we also look beyond the church. What is desperately needed in today's mainline churches is leaders who have a heart for gathering the unchurched, for inviting women and men into the sphere of God's grace as revealed in Jesus Christ, and for bearing a gracious witness to those who inhabit other religious traditions. There is no greater calling than to invite people to faith in the name of Jesus Christ.

Second, the church is identified with the *body of Christ*. Each member of the church, through baptism, has been united with Jesus' crucified, risen, and ascended body (Romans 6:3–5). What does it mean to be identified with Jesus' "body"? We catch a glimpse of this in the parable recorded in Matthew 25, where those gathered at the end of days learn of Jesus' concern for the "least of these," that is, the poor. Jesus tells them, "Truly I tell you, just as you did it to one of the least of these who are members of my family, you did it to me" (Matthew 25:40). Jesus' risen body, in other words, becomes a "real presence" to us in the bodies of the least, to whom we are called to minister. In the very next chapter of Matthew, Jesus' earthly body is anointed by an unnamed woman, and we are told that this act prefigures Jesus' burial (Matthew 26:6–13). In this story the woman—herself one of the least, herself a paradigm of the "church"—ministers to Jesus, who, in turn, through his crucifixion is going to become the very paradigm of the "least of these."

When read together, these stories tell us something profound. In ministering to one another in bodily, tangible ways, we identify with and minister unto Jesus; and in Jesus, we encounter the one who identifies with and ministers unto our bodily, tangible existence—even unto death. This is, I think, what Paul meant when he said that we share in the fellowship of his weakness, his vulnerability, his suffering (Philippians 3:10; Colossians 1:24). Thus, in the community we call the "body," no member is insignificant or unimportant. We laugh with those who laugh, we weep with those who weep (Romans 12:15). When one is in pain, all are in pain. And the alleviation of pain and suffering—both within the church and without—becomes one of the church's chief callings.

Third, the church is being knit together as a *fellowship of the Holy Spirit*. Just as the church was gathered by the Holy Spirit at Pentecost (Acts 2:1–47) and has been edified by the Spirit's gifts dispersed throughout the body (e.g., 1 Corinthians 12:1–31), so also by the same Spirit we are empowered to be witnesses to the gospel throughout the world (Acts 1:8). God sent the Spirit to minister to the church (e.g., John 14:26; Galatians 4:6; 1 Peter 1:12), and God also sends the church to minister to a world in need. We need to remember that just as the Spirit was present at creation (Genesis 1:2) and is at work through all the world (e.g., Psalm 139:7), so also we look for the Spirit to be at work—both in the church and outside the church. The Spirit who spoke through the mouths of the prophets calls all human beings to "do justice . . . love kindness, and . . . walk humbly with your God" (Micah 6:8). The fellowship of the Spirit is at work to knit human beings together in ways as diverse as the greatness of God's grace.

5. The church today faces the challenges and opportunities of a new postmodern, post-Christendom age.

For some time now the Western church has been moving into a new postmodern, post-Christendom situation.

Postmodernity is the intellectual situation that recognizes the achievements of the modern world but also its limitations and failings. Chastened by the many ways in which the modern world has let us down (two world wars, the advent of the nuclear age, the proliferation of genocide, the pervasiveness of global poverty, and the threat of environmental disaster), postmodernity has come to see all our thinking as contextually situated, fallible, and subject to revision. Although some forms of postmodernity call meaning and truth radically into question, more positive versions of postmodern sensibility may in fact prompt the church to recapture more authentic forms of Christian witness.

Similarly, post-Christendom is the social and cultural situation in which the Christian faith no longer forms the common presuppositions for Western society. It, too, challenges business as usual in the church. In the American context, the legal "disestablishment" of religion effected by the First Amendment has been matched by a gradual social and cultural disestablishment in recent decades. In the new post-Christendom era, the Western church can no longer rest on its laurels, simply assuming that the wider culture will automatically support Christian perspectives of what is true and right. In this new situation, catechesis within the church and evangelism outside the church take on a new urgency.

Yet it is a mistake to adopt a reactionary, circle-the-wagons stance towards these postmodern, post-Christendom developments. To do so is to fail to recognize that modernist forms of Christianity—e.g., both fundamentalism and liberalism—tend to reduce the gospel to a mere conceptual system. When one hears right-wing Christians claiming assuredly that their position is "biblical," this is often a coverup for a highly selective, conceptually grounded version of Christianity that is used to shore up the social and political status quo. Some left-wing versions of Christianity also play the game of picking and choosing from a list of Christian concepts in order to support positions that have originated from somewhere else.

Both liberals and conservatives in the church seem to long for the "good old days" when their versions of Christianity had more cultural credence in the world. This nostalgia fails to see that Christendom at its core was based on a fundamental sellout to imperial power. Ever since the Roman emperor Constantine converted to Christianity in the fourth century, the Western church has struck up a bargain whereby the secular authority supports the church in return for the church providing spiritual values for the broader society. Was this bargain in keeping with the *euangelion* of Jesus? Though this arrangement has benefited the church in some ways, it has not come without costs. One such cost is that the anti-imperial dimensions of the gospel (see thesis 1) have almost been lost from view.

The losses accruing to the church in the post-Christendom situation may also bring gains. Over time, in discovering new ways of being "church," we may discover more faithful ways of living out the gospel. Clearly, mainline religion has much to learn, but it also has much to contribute in this new situation. One of the historic strengths of the PC(USA) is its emphasis upon Bible and theology. This is just one of our contributions to the ecumenical church that needs to be preserved in the years ahead.

In response to the new postmodern, post-Christendom challenge, there have been many experiments in ecclesiology in recent years. In the 1990s some church leaders began jettisoning traditional symbols and practices in favor of strategies that were "seeker-friendly."[19] One result was the so-called megachurch. Today, early in the twenty-first century, others have become disillusioned with tightly drawn conceptions of Christian faith and are yearning for what they call an "emerging church," one that returns to the deepest wells of Christian tradition but moves beyond the confines of a narrow traditionalism.[20] What seems clear is that the bureaucratic model of church government, which thrived during the middle of the twentieth century, is less well suited to the new situation into which North American Christians are entering. The church needs once more to be open to the Spirit's leading and to see what new things God is doing in our time.

6. In our time, as has been true in all times, the God who is for *us and* with *us in Jesus Christ is calling us by the Spirit's power to be* for *and* with *each other.*

Our fidelity to the gospel is tested in the way we live. In particular it is tested in the way the gospel comes to expression in the fellowship of the church. We are united in baptism to many with whom we have differences. We are sustained by the bread and cup in a fellowship that is meant to express not the priorities of "conservative" or "liberal" ideology but the priorities of the reign of God.

Some say that the presenting issue before the church today—that is, the issue over which the church stands or falls—is human sexuality. In a world in which some 1.2 billion people live on less than $2.00 a day, this is an absurd claim. While the call to live a life of personal integrity is an important biblical priority, the remarkable preoccupation with sex in the American church represents a skewing of priorities. Ironically, conservatives and liberals agree on many things, such as that poverty is wrong. Working together, they could do much to make the world better and to further the aims of the gospel.[21]

The vital reality of the gospel is that God, in Jesus Christ, has reached out to embrace us because God loves us. This basic reality of grace is matched by the imperative God gives to the church today: "Go and do likewise" (Luke 10:37). Living out this reality and this imperative is what it means to be "church."

Questions for Discussion

1. How does the gospel come alive in your congregation? And how might what the gospel is doing in your midst call for ongoing reform of the church?

2. How does the fact that Jesus of Nazareth was tortured to death between two terrorists impact how you think about what the church is called to be and to do in the present day?

3. How might we reenvision the life and mission of the church so as to become more fully for and with one another?

Chapter 10

A Global Presbyterian Witness
for a Global World Community

Fahed Abu-Akel

As I write this essay, I am reflecting on my term of service from 2002 to 2003 as moderator of the 214th General Assembly of the Presbyterian Church (U.S.A.) and the events in my life that brought me to that point. It was an amazing whirlwind experience for me and put me into a role never imagined, but one undergirded by the spiritual and practical strength of incredibly helpful colleagues in Christ.

As I worked with the commissioners through the platform docket and moved into the follow-up phase of my duties as General Assembly moderator, four important issues for our denomination emerged: spiritual renewal, local and global mission, unity in the midst of our diversity, and hospitality. Now, two years later, these four areas of concern still seem to me to be key agenda for PC(USA) congregations. In my estimation they deserve even greater emphasis now than before. Let me give some reasons from my personal experience and perspective.

Radical changes in our world challenge us to review the historic role of Presbyterians within the Reformed tradition and our place as members of the church universal. These winds of change rattle our stained-glass windows and threaten the comfort of our pews and plans. But we must not forget that the wind of the Holy Spirit also blows. That wind can give us the mind of Christ to guide and serve our church and generation faithfully. Technology, a growing global economy, and a world punctuated by major hot spots of conflict, terrorism, hunger, and recent natural disasters demand that we listen better to the Holy Spirit if we hope to meet both the obvious and the unforeseen challenges of the real world in which we live.

The action of the 216th General Assembly (2004) with regard to Israel/ Palestine reveals that the influence of our denomination is far greater than our size might indicate. Subsequent action by the World Council of Churches commended our approach to the Middle East conflict to its 347 member bodies in

120 countries. Anglican and other mainstream voices have already embraced the methods and rationale we set forth—all of which indicates a significant spiritual and moral consensus joining with us to address situations "on the ground" in the Middle East and around the globe. We Presbyterians can be "decent and in order" and at the same time influential and effective in bringing about constructive change! Now let me share with you my thoughts on these priority areas of our church life—spiritual renewal, local and global mission, unity in the midst of our diversity, and hospitality—and on peacemaking.

Spiritual Renewal

Presbyterians in the twenty-first century must teach the basic tenets of the Christian faith based on our Reformed theology. In Austin, Texas, a 45-year-old man asked the associate pastor in the new membership class, "What is Easter and what is the resurrection?" Such questions point to several priority areas for our ministry and mission in what I would describe as a post-Christian America.

1. *Christian education.* We must teach the basic doctrines of our Reformed, Trinitarian faith about God, Jesus Christ, the Holy Spirit, sin, salvation, and how to grow spiritually in our personal and corporate faith. We need to move our people from an American "cultural Christianity" to a relevant New Testament expression of Christian discipleship. To accomplish this will require a vigorous emphasis on biblical literacy. Without a core of basic Bible knowledge, sermons and church school lessons will make little sense and spiritual growth will be limited.

2. *Reading and studying the* Book of Order. The Constitution of our church includes the Bible, the *Book of Confessions* and the *Book of Order.* The *Book of Order* is not just for ministers of the Word and Sacrament, elders, and deacons, but should inform every member of our congregations. The first four chapters alone constitute a rich primer of our Presbyterian faith and heritage. Our people need familiarity with how and why we do what we do. Knowing the Constitution of the PC(USA) is a part of equipping the saints.

3. *The priesthood of all believers and the importance of lay ministry.* In the Reformed tradition, ministry and mission belong to all members of the body of Christ, not just those who are set apart by ordination for specific functions. The theology of the priesthood of all believers is very important to our branch of Protestantism. Engaging every person in the meaningful discovery of his or her gifts and Christian vocation assures an outgrowth of mission and ministry both within the walls of the church and into the community and world as we are commissioned to do. But there is another important aspect we must not miss. I can be your priest, and you can be mine; but I cannot be my own priest,

nor you yours. That demands a relationship that brings us into a healthy fellowship in need of each other. Spiritual renewal is realized when we go beyond just listening and learning, and put our faith into action where we live and work as well as where we go. Doing the work of the church is commendable, but true leadership involves enabling all to serve and enjoy participation in the gospel.

Local and Global Mission

The invitation to each elder and member is to be involved in a local or global mission project that will help our people to be renewed spiritually. We need to challenge our members to experience the global church, to see how God is moving by the Spirit in Latin America, Africa, the Middle East, Europe, and Asia. Today, the Presbyterian Church is growing all over the world but not in the United States. Why? We Westerners in North America must learn from our mission partners in eighty nations why this growth is taking place and learn from them new ways our church can grow. Living in the strongest military, economic, educational, and research nation does not guarantee spiritual renewal. We must humble ourselves and learn from our mission church partners new ways that God is working in Jesus Christ in these nations.

Our pastors and elders can help our members see that mission is done through effective partnership. The old colonial mission mentality is over. Change in global politics, commerce, and technology is happening faster than we have admitted as a church. The implications for our approach to the world in obedience to the Great Commission must be faced and prayerfully studied. Thank God for our missionaries and the Worldwide Ministries Division that help us recognize and respond to this fact. We can be thankful for the rich heritage of Presbyterian mission work in prior centuries, but we must also humbly and gratefully receive the reciprocal ministry and renewal these partner churches offer us in a new century and a changing world. We need the ministry and priesthood of our partnership churches, and they cannot do without the same from us. As a connectional church we must maintain these essential linkages given the body of Christ in the will and plan of God. Moreover, we need to communicate this phenomenon of worldwide church growth to all of our members.

Throughout the history of our mission activity around the world, we have emphasized these areas:

1. *Evangelism.* We believe that every person around the world should be invited to believe and accept Jesus Christ as the Savior and Lord in their lives. As a result of that clear focus on the mandate of the gospel of Jesus Christ, today we have mission partners in eighty nations, and Reformed and Presbyterian churches are growing faster in Africa, Asia, and Latin America than in

the United States and Europe. Today there are fifteen million Arab Christians in the Middle East who can trace their traditions back to the day of Pentecost. Among these are more than a half million Arab Presbyterians, as a result of our mission work dating back as early as 1823.

2. *Medical missions.* Presbyterians have always cared for the whole person in our mission work. In the Bible the person is a unity of body, mind, and spirit. We are called to minister to every aspect of the image of God that we are created to be. Thus we have established clinics and hospitals and have trained doctors and nurses to care for and to love all people in the name of Jesus Christ.

3. *Education.* In every nation where we have established missions, education has been a priority. We established schools, colleges, universities, and seminaries because we believe that education is basic to spreading the gospel and learning about Jesus Christ, who himself ministered to the whole person. Education leads to giving others a saving knowledge of Jesus Christ as the light of the world. Historically God has blessed Presbyterians in a unique way because of our faithfulness to Jesus' mandate to "go and make disciples of all nations . . . teaching them to observe all that I have commanded you." In the twenty-first century, obedience to this mandate will continue our rich tradition in mission work.

I salute each of our PC(USA) congregations that is involved in local and global mission. Without mission, the church cannot survive. Mission is at the heartbeat of God. Throughout history God has spoken to his people through the prophets and through the written word of God, and finally God came to us in Jesus Christ two thousand years ago. In the incarnation, Jesus, Emmanuel, is God with us. God loved the human family so much that he came to us in Jesus Christ. The message of God to the world through the church must be to proclaim the birth, life, ministry, mission, death on the cross, resurrection from the dead, and the reality of the coming again of Jesus Christ.

Unity in the Midst of Our Diversity

As Presbyterians, we talk a lot and like to discuss every issue that we face as individuals, families, and a denomination, in our congregations, communities, nation, and world. Our Reformed theology helps us to do that. Our differences must never outweigh what we hold in common. We should not become so wrapped up in single issues that we fail to see the whole picture. We must serve all to properly serve any, but in every generation we face new and sensitive issues that relate to our theology, our practice, and the biblical witness. The stress of these newly emerging issues can make us or break us.

One especially great problem that we and our sister denominations face today is how to deal with the divisiveness raised by gay and lesbian constituents and their supporters. In our case, a small minority has sought to impose its will on the majority of the PC(USA). Our leaders must focus on our unity in the midst of those issues that divide us. I hope and pray that the great majority of Presbyterians will not allow those on either side of the issues concerning gay and lesbian persons, or any other such issue, to cripple the life and mission of the PC(USA). While we should never ignore the voice and concerns of the minority, we must trust the Holy Spirit's guidance of the whole.

Hospitality

Beyond the general hospitality we share in the fellowship of our congregations and communities, there are specific opportunities. For example, I serve as executive director of the Atlanta Ministry with International Students and the national director of the Christmas International House. The twenty-two colleges in greater Atlanta have more than 8,000 international students from 150 nations. In 2004, nationwide there were 572,000 international students and scholars from 190 nations. In U.S. colleges and universities we educate one million people from other countries with BAs, master's, PhDs, and other research degrees every ten years. These are the future political, economic, social, educational, and religious leaders of their own nations.

Hospitality opens hearts and doors, bonds strangers in friendship, and brings lifelong benefits to all. Hospitality is a Christian virtue and a practice urged upon the early church. Through the gift of friendship and hospitality Presbyterians have an opportunity to serve and to obey our Lord in a way that sows seeds of peace and understanding. I challenge each congregation to get involved with a nearby college and to extend the hand of friendship and hospitality to international students in our midst.

Through Christmas International House, I invite congregations to host five to ten students over the Christmas holiday each year. This ministry with international students is for the moment, at least, the best mission field at our doorsteps in the United States. Opening the Internet at www.christmasih.org will inform individuals and congregations about how to engage in this vital ministry.

We all know that the urban landscape of America has already changed. We live in a more pluralistic world than we have ever known. We have new immigrants in our midst from every nation under the sun. I challenge each congregation to see this new reality as an opportunity for mission, and not as a threat. Let us move in the Spirit of Christ and his gospel command and reach out to welcome these new immigrants and visitors to worship and to our homes.

May God help all of us to learn the joy of God's gift of hospitality, which is the best tool of evangelism, to welcome new people into our churches, and there to discover the risen Christ.

Peacemaking and Presbyterians

At the beginning of this chapter I pointed out the signal role of Presbyterians in addressing the injustices that have reached the saturation point in the part of the world from which I come, that Christians, Jews, and Muslims everywhere identify as the Holy Land and Christians acknowledge as the birthplace of Jesus, our Lord. While we must never neglect those suffering from the heinous atrocities occurring in places like the Sudan and, earlier, in Rwanda and in other countries, I am convinced that the ethnic cleansing and the linkages worldwide to the declared and hidden goals of the political powers in the Middle East, including the United States, are not only a physical and economic logjam but have held our world in spiritual captivity. We need to look for solutions rather than blame. I must reiterate the importance of our involvement and make a plea for us to renew our identity as peacemakers and reconcilers.

The Hunger Program of the General Assembly has matched the Presbytery of Greater Atlanta with Palestine in a program called Joining Hands against Hunger in Palestine. For the last three years, members of this task force have visited the West Bank, Jerusalem, and Gaza and have hosted Palestinians in Atlanta. Through our relationship, we have discovered that hunger as a result of occupation has become a crisis in Palestine. According to a recent study at the United Nations, more than half of Palestinians now live on less than $2.00 a day.

The bold step of the 216th General Assembly (2004) toward peacemaking in the longstanding Israel/Palestinian conflict must not fail. As North American Christians, we live in the most powerful nation on earth. We are powerful militarily, economically, technologically, and educationally. In light of this enormous power, the church in the United States must take the humble way or the Jesus way, focusing on peacemaking and reconciliation in our own lives, in our families, and in our churches, community, nation, and world. Our emphasis as believers on peacemaking gives credibility to the power of the gospel in a secular world that loves war and violence more than peace. Jesus said, "Blessed are the peacemakers, for they will be called children of God" (Matthew 5:9).

In his book *Justice and Only Justice*, the Rev. Naim Ateek as a Palestinian Christian shares the story of how his village was destroyed in 1948. Ateek, through calling attention to key passages in the Old and New Testaments, helps the reader focus on the biblical demands of justice. The call of Micah 6:8, "to do justice, and to love kindness, and to walk humbly with your God," is key to our biblical teaching.

We can justifiably celebrate the 216th General Assembly action concerning the Palestinian/Israeli conflict. We want to thank our denomination, and especially the General Assembly, for focusing our attention in the last few years by passing resolutions addressing the following aspects of the Palestine question.

1. *The occupation.* The Israeli military occupation, disrupting the lives of four million Palestinian Arab Christians and Muslims, must end. Since 1967, the Israeli military has been occupying the West Bank, East Jerusalem, and Gaza in defiance of international law. We say that the occupation must end because it is oppressive, inhuman, and inhumane. For the last thirty-nine years, the Palestinian people have had no freedom or liberty, which is the entitlement of every human being. Moreover, this occupation has meant confiscation and annexation of land, which is squeezing life from the rightful owners.

2. *The Wall.* Israel continues to build the Wall on Palestinian land against the will of the United Nations and of the international community. The Wall is built to prevent Palestinian terrorists from entering Israel and to protect illegal Israeli Jewish settlements built inside the Palestinian lands. One million Palestinians are cut off from their own land, deprived of access to jobs, schools, hospitals, and places of worship. The International Court of Justice ruled that the Wall is illegal and must be torn down, and even the Israeli Supreme Court said that part of the Wall around Bethlehem is illegal and must be stopped. I salute this General Assembly for its prophetic stand against the Wall.

3. *Christian Zionism.* We Presbyterians say that theology matters. In our Reformed theology, we do not accept the dispensational or premillennialist theology propounded by Darby and Scofield, which teaches that history is divided into seven dispensational periods and that the creation of the political state of Israel in 1948 marks one of those periods. This doctrine, harking back to late nineteenth- and early twentieth-century teachings, has now created a division in Christendom and feeds into the present crisis in the Middle East.

With the creation of the state of Israel, Christian Zionists believe that the clock is now ticking fast toward the battle of Armageddon, the thousand-year rule of Christ, and the end of time, and that Israel must ultimately control not only the West Bank, but also the land between the River Nile of Egypt and the Euphrates River of Iraq for God's plan to be fulfilled. So the presence of Palestinian Arab Christians and Arab Muslims in Palestine is viewed as a hindrance to the will of God.

Many so-called and self-identified evangelical or fundamentalist denominations, along with highly visible spokespersons like Pat Robertson and Jerry Falwell, preach this theology on TV and with books like *The Late Great Planet Earth* by Hal Lindsey and the Left Behind series of Tim LaHaye and Jerry B. Jenkins. Sold all over America, these books are based on a bloody theology that sanctions ethnic cleansing to enable God's plan to be fulfilled in Palestine. We Presbyterians do not accept this theology as being either biblical or

Reformed. We have to state this clearly and help our people work for justice and peace between Israeli Jews and Palestinian Arabs, rather than helping them kill each other.

4. *The phased selective divestment policy.* Thank God for the elders, ministers, and sessions that took this resolution to the Presbytery of St. Augustine; thank God for the Presbytery of St. Augustine, which sent the overture to the 216th General Assembly; and thank God for the commissioners to the 216th General Assembly for their prophetic stand for justice and peace between Israeli Jews and Palestinian Arabs. The PC(USA) divestment policy is neither anti-Jewish nor anti-Israel nor anti-Semitic. Rather, our policy is "antioccupation." Our implementation of this step is studied, deliberate, and fair. Its provisions protect against using an unjust means to fight injustice.

The Presbyterian Church has been a friend of Israel from day one in 1948. Today more Jewish synagogues hold their Friday Sabbath worship services in Presbyterian sanctuaries than in sanctuaries of any other Protestant denomination in the United States. Jews and Presbyterians have long worked together to end racism in the United States and have worked for social justice and civil and human rights as leaders in our communities. American Jews and Presbyterians worked together effectively to oppose the apartheid system in South Africa. Today American Jews and Presbyterians must continue to work together for justice and peace for both Israeli Jews and Palestinian Arabs. We both know the basic facts on the ground in the West Bank—that occupation of the Palestinian people and Palestinian land is a key issue that must be resolved very soon. Peace can never be possible for either party if it is not possible for both parties.

America, the friend of Israel, helped make peace between Israel and Egypt. America helped Israel make peace with Jordan. I believe in coming days we can help Israel make peace with Syria, Lebanon, Iraq, Saudi Arabia, and every other Arab country. But if we fail to make peace between Israeli Jews and Palestinian Arabs, we will fail with our policy in the Middle East. The sooner we do justice to the Palestinians, to enable them to gain their freedom and to establish an independent Palestinian state in the West Bank, Gaza, and East Jerusalem, the sooner our nation will build credibility in the Middle East and around the world.

Beyond the foregoing matters, which seem self-evident, lies the plight of Israeli Arab citizens—Christians, Druzes, Muslims, and Bedouins who remained in the borders of the newly formed Israeli state in 1948. Theirs is a story that needs to be understood and addressed as well. All are affected. It is out of that particular Palestinian population that my own story emerged.

I grew up in a village twenty-five miles northwest of Nazareth in the Galilee of Palestine. I am grateful that my father and mother, five sisters, and two brothers helped me to be nurtured in the Christian faith. My native church was Eastern Orthodox, harking back to the original church established in the fourth century under Constantine. Worship was in the Greek Orthodox form. But it was my mother whose own beautiful tradition was to help us children to pray, to memorize and to recite the Psalms, the Gospels, the Lord's Prayer, and the Nicene Creed before we went to sleep.

As a four-year-old child, I still remember leaving home with my father, five sisters, and two brothers and leaving our mother at home alone. We went up to the mountains to a Druze Arab village called Yrka, and there we were put in a makeshift Palestinian refugee camp in tents. We stayed several months and then went back home to find my mother alive, but the new Israeli army had destroyed four nearby Palestinian Arab villages.

When Israel became a state on May 14, 1948, it was a day of celebration and independence to the Jewish people of Palestine, but a day of *nakba* or catastrophe and destruction to the indigenous Arab Palestinian population. On the land where Israel became a state, 418 Palestinian Arab Christian and Muslim villages and towns were destroyed, and more than 800,000 displaced Palestinian Arab Christians and Muslims were exiled and forced to move from their homes, lands, businesses, and places of worship. The issues of the right of Palestinians to return and the threat of transfer out of Israel to those holding citizenship must be brought before the world tribunal.

From this early beginning, through the grace of God and guidance of the Holy Spirit, I encountered two Scottish Presbyterian missionaries who came to live on the second floor of our home. How grateful to God I am for Dr. Doris Wilson and Ruth Lenox. Dr. Wilson helped me to give my life to Jesus Christ and became my spiritual mentor as I received my call to the ministry. With their encouragement I arrived in the United States on January 29, 1966, in Tampa, Florida, with one suitcase, one Arabic Bible, and an English-Arabic dictionary to pursue my education and to begin my new American journey.

I received my BA degree from Southeastern University in Lakeland, Florida, and went on to receive a Master of Divinity degree from Columbia Seminary in Decatur, Georgia. I began my ministry at First Presbyterian Church in Atlanta, working with the children in the community and the youth of that great congregation. I was ordained and installed in 1978, becoming a minister of the Word and Sacrament in the Presbyterian Church U.S. and a member of the Presbytery of Greater Atlanta. Thus equipped and encouraged, I started the ecumenical ministry called the Atlanta Ministry with International Students. Thirty-six years after my arrival on these shores, I was elected as the 214th moderator of the General Assembly of the Presbyterian Church (U.S.A.).

As a grateful immigrant to these United States, every year I celebrate my personal "July 4th" four times: (1) January 29, the date I arrived in the United States; (2) March 10, the day I became an American citizen; (3) June 15, the day I was elected as moderator of the 214th General Assembly in Columbus, Ohio; and (4) July 4, when, along with all my fellow Americans, I too celebrate our Independence Day!

Where in all the world can a Palestinian Arab Christian who almost became a refugee—but was then nurtured by his Christian mother in the faith and witnessed to by two Scottish Presbyterian missionaries, who led him to come to the United States to study—thirty-six years later find himself elected to the highest position in his denomination? This could happen only in the church of Jesus Christ, and, in my case, only in our beloved Presbyterian Church (U.S.A.), and it could happen only in the United States.

My prayer for our beloved denomination and all believers is that we may together live and move and act obediently on the grace, mercy, and peace of our Lord and Savior Jesus Christ as we boldly embrace the future God has set before us.

Questions for Discussion

1. What are the ways that your congregation relates to the larger church and its mission—presbytery, synod, General Assembly, other?
2. Does your congregation equip its members for their ministries in the everyday world? If so, how?
3. What are some concrete ways that you and your congregation can support peacemaking in the church and the world?

Chapter 11

The Presbyterian Church of 2050

Scott D. Anderson

> Go therefore and make disciples of all nations, baptizing them in the
> name of the Father and of the Son and of the Holy Spirit, and teaching
> them to obey everything that I have commanded you. And remember, I
> am with you always, to the end of the age.
>
> *Matthew 28:19–20*

*L*ast spring on the twenty-five-minute puddle-jumper flight between O'Hare
Airport in Chicago and Madison, I sat next to an elderly woman, a United
Methodist from Portage, Wisconsin. We started talking about the church, and
she asked me, "Why is it that we Methodists say 'trespasses' in the Lord's
Prayer while you Presbyterians say 'debts'?"

We covered lots of territory in the brief conversation that ensued. We talked
about the way the New Testament is translated, reviewed a little church history, then focused on the ecumenical version of the Lord's Prayer, which I
believe is really the best translation: "Forgive us our sins, as we forgive those
who sin against us."

While my Methodist seatmate nodded approval, the young high school
senior from Madison next to her in the window seat looked dazed. As our
plane landed, she asked, "What exactly is the Lord's Prayer?"

I sat in stunned silence. How could anyone not know about the Lord's
Prayer? And then I felt flush with embarrassment. It was as if the Methodist
and the Presbyterian had enjoyed an insider twenty-minute discussion about
baseball, insensitive to our seatmate who didn't really know anything about
the game itself.

The high school student's innocent question was a telling reminder to me
of the sea change taking place in American culture. The United States no
longer reflects the ethos of mainstream Protestant Christianity, at least in the
way you and I were raised to believe it does, or think it should. The Lutheran

across the street, the Episcopalian next door, and the Roman Catholic who lives down on the corner aren't present in the way they were fifty years ago.

Most of our neighbors, in fact, have no church affiliation, and an increasing number, like the young woman in the window seat, have had absolutely no experience or contact with the institutional church. More important, the saving message of the gospel of Jesus Christ is not being heard.

While our culture has changed, the Presbyterian Church, like all of the mainline denominations, continues to focus on an insider discussion about baseball as if the culture will understand. When I go to meetings of our General Assembly, and I have gone to many over the last twenty-five years, it seems that we are either grieving because things are not what they used to be, or we are busy trying to recreate the greatness of glory days gone by.

What does the Presbyterian Church need today? Let's not focus on our current challenges: declining membership, perpetual conflict, and our marginalization in the wider culture. Let's not spin our wheels trying to relive what once was and will never be again. Instead, let's allow God's Spirit to work through us and imagine a new future: What will the Presbyterian Church (U.S.A.) look like in the year 2050?

The sobering reality is that most Presbyterians who are alive today will not be here in 2050, and those of us who are here will not be in charge. New people will be joining our churches, serving on our sessions, and leading the denomination—new people who have grown up in a culture very different from the one you and I have known.

A Missionary Movement

The first thing I imagine about 2050 is that the institutional form of the Presbyterian Church will not be a national bureaucracy but rather a missionary movement. The private sector abandoned the bureaucratic model more than twenty years ago. The public sector is busy reinventing itself, though having a more difficult time letting go of old patterns. I imagine that the church of 2050 will look less like the corporation of the mid-twentieth century and more like the missionary church described in the New Testament. It will be more organic and less mechanistic, more of a network than a structure, more decentralized, more fluid, flexible, responsive, and accountable to local needs. It will feel more like a movement, less like an institution.

By 2050 the Presbyterian Church as a missionary movement will be completely focused on *making disciples*. Because the institutional church as we know it today will not survive in the next five decades, "institutional survival" will no longer be our explicit or implicit goal. The proclamation of the gospel will be the church's overriding passion, and by 2050 the Presbyterian Church will be blessed with new organizational forms that will be enable it to act on this missional imperative within our mid-twenty-first-century non-Christian culture.

The primary mission field of the Presbyterian Church in 2050 will not be Ghana, Brazil, or Korea. It will be our unchurched neighbors here in the United States. Our nineteenth- and twentieth-century zeal for sending mission workers to the far corners of the globe will be replaced with our twenty-first-century zeal for receiving missionaries from the burgeoning churches in Africa, Asia, and South America. Their success in making disciples within a non-Christian context will be indispensable for the Presbyterian Church's new priority of homeland mission.

Missionally Engaged with the World

The second thing I imagine about the church of 2050 is that it will not reside in subcultural ghettos but will be missionally engaged with the multicultural realities of the new century. In our denomination, the ethnic homogeneity of Scottish Presbyterians at the birth of this nation has given way to the new subcultural ghetto of white middle- and upper-middle-class suburbia, which is where the Presbyterian Church now does best.

The hard news about this imagining is that thousands of existing Presbyterian congregations will no longer exist, mostly in the depopulated rural parts of America. If you live in an agricultural community, you know exactly what I'm talking about. The kids grow up, graduate from high school, and leave town, never to return home. The family farm system of the nineteenth century has given way to modern agribusiness. There are just too many churches for fewer and fewer people, and many of our country and small town congregations will close in the next five decades.

The good news about this imagining is that new church plants will be succeeding in the burgeoning supermetropolises of the twenty-first century, such as Chicago, Minneapolis, and Atlanta. New Presbyterian congregations will take root and bear fruit with young singles and elderly Gen X-ers, among gays and lesbians forming families and raising children, in the urban core as well as in middle-class suburbs, among African Americans, Asian Americans, Hispanics, and second- and third-generation immigrants. The missionary zeal of the 2050 church to *make disciples of all nations* will help heal the racism, classism, and homophobia that today keeps us stuck in our mainline subcultural ghettos.

Presbyterian congregations, which will be the heart and soul of our 2050 church, will look different from the way they look today. As the national church took a bureaucratic form in the twentieth century, so congregations often resembled the local franchises of the modern corporation, complete with a board of directors (the session), bylaws, committees, salaried managers (pastors), and a market-savvy location for business (church property). The economics of the local franchise—the congregation's ability to pay a full-time, salaried pastor along with owning property—defined the viability of the local church.

This will change in the next fifty years. The viability of the 2050 congregation will not be driven by its ability to pay a full-time pastor or own property, but rather by its commitment to engage in the mission of making disciples. The work of the congregation will be shaped by the needs of those who are not yet part of the congregation and not exclusively by the needs of the current membership. A full-time salaried pastor may be the exception to the 2050 norm of "tent-making" Presbyterian evangelists (following the example of the apostle Paul, a church leader who holds down a secular job in addition to carrying out churchly responsibilities), and nonordained staff with specialized skills. Members of the congregation will be empowered to carry out many of the functions that salaried pastors perform today. The entire educational infrastructure of the denomination—particularly its seminaries—will be utterly transformed to meet the needs of this new, missional focus of the local church.

Worship, education, evangelism, and decision making in congregations will all look different in fifty years. Presbyterian worship will be far livelier than it is today, and the cradle-to-grave educational ministry of the church will employ the best of the current technological tools. Evangelism—the 2050 church's primary focus—will be rooted in a ministry of hospitality to our unchurched neighbors, inviting them into a new kind of community where Christ welcomes all. Committees will give way to more organic decision-making structures, with groups of people forming and reforming to accomplish specific tasks and to envision new directions. Instead of owning property, the 2050 Presbyterian congregation will more likely lease building space, moving several times in the course of its life to meet changing needs or to reach new populations.

A New Meaning for Baptism

My third imagining is that the meaning of *baptism* will take on new importance for Presbyterians of the mid-twenty-first century. In the twentieth century, many of us lived as if our gender were our primary identity. Some of us thought our ethnicity is what primarily shaped our selfhood. Still others of us focused on our sexual orientation—being gay or lesbian, or heterosexual. Many of us thought our economic station in life, being well off—or even our nation of residence, being "American"—is what mattered most about who we were.

For Presbyterians of 2050, their primary identity will be "Christian," and Christian identity comes through baptism. Unlike the twentieth century, when baptism was reduced to a warm, fuzzy one-time ritual involving young parents and their newborn child, baptismal identity in 2050 will move to the center of the church's ministry. It will organize and prioritize all other facets of our private and public lives, and shape our self-identity more than gender, more than race, more than sexual orientation, more than economic status or country of residence.

The reclamation of our baptismal identity in the twenty-first century will bring peace to the sexuality wars of the twentieth. Heterosexual marriage, which was in shambles at the close of the last century, the exponential rise in teenage pregnancy, the debate over the sanctity of same-gender relationships, and the onslaught of a secular culture obsessed with sex will all find a remedy in the ancient initiation rite of Christian baptism. The only "lifestyle" 2050 Christians will be concerned about is the lifestyle of discipleship, which is shaped by the "one flesh" union Christians have with Christ and is sealed in our baptism. That union—our primary identity as a part of the body of Christ—will inform and shape all other identities.

Christian baptism does three things with respect to sexuality. First, it makes our sexuality the gift and responsibility of the community and not an individual entitlement or a privacy issue between consenting adults. Child rearing, mutual support in good times and bad, and dealing with irreconcilable differences are communal responsibilities and have communal impact.

Second, baptism reminds us that promise making and promise keeping are central to our union with Christ and the unions we form with each other. The 2050 church will take much more seriously the public promises that are made: the promise of a couple to fidelity and to mutual accountability, and the promises of the community to support each couple.

Third, mirroring the "one flesh" union of Christ with the church, the 2050 church will openly challenge its members to restrict sexual activity to relationships that embody lifelong commitment and faithfulness.

One final word about the baptismal perspective of the 2050 church: our union with the body of Christ as our primary identifier will open the door to the recognition and blessing of same-gender partnerships. All Christians—gay or straight—will be subject to the same set of sexual ethics, rooted in our Christian baptism.

A New Approach to Other Faiths

Another imagining I have about the church of 2050 is that it will have a different relationship with people of other faiths. To be *baptized in the name of the Father and of the Son and of the Holy Spirit* will take on new meaning and importance.

Our Christian identity will exist in an ever-shrinking, religiously pluralistic world, calling the Presbyterian Church of the twenty-first century to a new kind of relationship with other religious traditions. In conflict zones throughout the world today—Northern Ireland, the Balkans, Chechnya, Tajikistan, the Middle East, Sudan, Sri Lanka, India, Kashmir, and East Timor—religious difference is on the cutting edge of confrontation. I'm reminded of Jonathan Swift's acid observation that we have just enough religion to make us hate one another, and not enough to make us love one another.

By 2050 the name "Christian" will not be a threat to people of other faiths. It will no longer be identified with Western imperialism, and it will make truth claims about the God we know as Father, Son, and Holy Spirit in a way that actively and thoughtfully engages the truth claims of the world's religions. Christian faith in 2050 will be deepened by interreligious dialogue, not compromised by it.

The Presbyterians of 2050 will reclaim the heart and soul of Christian discipleship, which is loving God and loving neighbor as oneself. Their Christian witness to people of other faith traditions will be rooted in the self-giving love they know in Jesus Christ, not through conquest, not through dogmatic triumphalism, and not as an instrument of any nation's foreign policy. They will form caring and respectful relationships with their Muslim neighbors, Jewish friends, Hindu classmates, and work associates who practice Native American spirituality. And they will live in the religiously pluralistic world of 2050 with the kind of humility and self-confidence that comes through trust in a sovereign God who may indeed be actively at work in others outside the Christian family.

Toward a More Biblically Centered, Countercultural Witness

My final imagining is that the cultural captivity of the twentieth-century church will give way to a more biblically centered, countercultural form of Christian witness. Jesus not only commissioned his followers to make disciples of all nations, baptizing them in the name of the Father, Son, and Holy Spirit, but also to *teach them to obey everything he has commanded.*

I imagine this to mean, first and foremost, that we ordinary Presbyterians will know a lot more about the Bible than we do today. In the twentieth century, those of us in the pews literally gave the Bible away. First we gave it away to the academy—colleges and seminaries—believing that those with "PhD" after their names were the only ones who were capable of understanding and interpreting the Scriptures. Seminary professors, and their students who are now our pastors, became the living repository of biblical schol-arship, while most of us Presbyterian pew-sitters self-identified as biblically and theologically inferior.

I imagine the Presbyterian Church of 2050 will be a lot less enamored with the culturally captive approach of credentialing the professionals, and a lot more enamored with the countercultural, biblically rooted approach of equip-ping the saints—all the saints—for ministry. Lay people are going to become far more important in the church of 2050, as the distance between the ordained and the nonordained shrinks dramatically. A seminary education in 2050 will not be offered only for "the professionals." It will be available to every Pres-byterian in radically new, not yet imagined ways.

In the twentieth century first we gave the Bible away to the academy. Then we gave the Bible away to another group of Christians who have come to be known as the Religious Right. Ask most Americans today who are the "Bible-believing Christians," and they will invariably point to Christian evangelicals and television preachers. Presbyterians are not on that list. We gave the Bible away to the Religious Right, and they willingly took up the cause of pro-claiming their version of biblical truth as if it represented us all.

Teach them to obey everything I have commanded you. I imagine that to mean that the Presbyterian Church of 2050, by reclaiming the Bible for all its members, will be unapologetically prophetic. It will model what community should really be about, critique all the false gods of the world, and engage the civic society about the dehumanizing ways it treats its most vulnerable citi-zens. In the twentieth-century church, we tried to do that by issuing bold pro-nouncements to government, believing that a democratic government in a Christian society would listen to what we had to say.

The Presbyterian Church of 2050 will not be so naive. I imagine that it will practice a more effective kind of civic engagement at the grassroots level, focused on developing relationships with civic leaders rather than in making public pronouncements. The twenty-first-century church will implement what our Lutheran brothers and sisters call "communities of moral deliberation." Congregations that are communities of moral deliberation are safe places to explore the great issues of our day. Here we can agree to disagree, because what binds us together is deeper than our differences. Here Scripture and the daily news intersect in the process of Christian formation. Here our local church leaders ask not, "How many members will we lose if we talk about this hot button issue?" but rather "What is faithfulness to the gospel at this moment of history?"

I am one who believes that the future of the Presbyterian Church (U.S.A.) looks brighter than yesteryear. That future is primarily dependent upon the providence of God, but also on our ability to be radically open to new possibilities as the Spirit leads. In the Scriptures, change is rarely incremental, and it is never pain-free. Jesus, in giving his disciples the Great Commission, anticipated their fear and reluctance to embrace a new future. So he promises: *Remember, I am with you always, to the end of the age*. That promise is still with us. It is the salve that heals our fears that the future will be different from the past, and is the ground of our hope that our best days are not behind us, but lie ahead.

> God is. We are. In spite of our fumbles and because of God's grace, we are not daunted by the troubles of this age, nor are we fearful of what is to come. We do not bless God for our wealth, or health or our feeble wisdom. We bless God that God is, that we are and that God's promise and love shall be with us when time itself will be no more.[1]
>
> *Peter Gomes*

Questions for Discussion

1. Do you believe that the church as we know it will be radically different in 2050? Describe its characteristics.
2. Will our primary mission field in 2050 be the United States? Will the nations to whom we have sent missionaries in the past send missionaries to the United States? Will we still need to send missionaries to other countries?
3. Do you believe that the pastoral norm for congregations in 2050 will be pastors who hold down full- or part-time jobs outside of the congregation? What difference would that make in the life of your congregation?

Chapter 12

What the Church Needs Today

Michael R. Walker

As a young person with a passion for Christ, when I think about what the church needs today, I want to say something radical. I want to be an uncompromising activist, a true believer, and speak a word that will cause alarm and raise hackles. I have felt this way ever since I became a Christian at age fifteen, while reading the Gospel of John. I have wanted to speak this way precisely because this was how I heard Jesus speak to the first disciples and to would-be first-century believers throughout that Gospel. And this is how I heard Jesus speak to me.

In part because I did not grow up in the Presbyterian Church—or any church, for that matter—my experience of faith in Christ was startling, new, and calling for serious change. Having been in the Presbyterian Church for only seven years now, and having been thrust into the center of denominational renewal efforts and controversies, my experience is still, in many ways, startling, new, and calling for serious change.

There are good things about this "relative newcomer" status. I am not jaded. Losing a passion for the truth or for the church is not an immediate temptation. And though I could probably be pegged pretty easily on matters of denominational controversy, I hope to engage those topics in atypical ways. Yet my study of history keeps me from being naive. There are no easy solutions to our needs. Indeed, the solution to our most basic need, our need to be reconciled to the almighty and triune God of the universe, was not an easy solution.

We must begin with that most radical and wrenching of all answers when we think about the most pressing questions before the church today. We must begin with the cross of Jesus Christ, a truly alarming solution to a truly drastic need. To speak of the cross as a "solution" may not be the best way to put it, theologically accurate though it may be. We might better call it the *path*, the *journey*, the *way* of our salvation.

Putting it this way captures the historic and ever-challenging Reformed emphasis on the cross, not only as the substitutionary sacrifice through which Christ accomplished the forgiveness of sins, but also the road of self-denial to which he has called all his followers, from the first-century believers to the twenty-first-century Presbyterians. The great Reformer John Calvin, never known for mincing words, puts it this way:

> For even though that Son was beloved above the rest, and in him the Father's mind was well pleased, yet we see that far from being treated indulgently or softly, to speak the truth, while he dwelt on earth he was not only tried by a perpetual cross but his whole life was nothing but a sort of perpetual cross. Why should we exempt ourselves, therefore, from the condition to which Christ our Head had to submit, especially since he submitted to it for our sake to show us an example of patience in himself? Therefore, the apostle teaches that God has destined all his children to the end that they be conformed to Christ (Romans 8:29).[1]

Elsewhere Calvin describes the essence of discipleship this way: "The sum of the Christian life is self-denial."[2]

To be honest, some days the truth that the cross is the shape of our salvation—both our justification and our sanctification—strikes me as just another theological truth, and on those days it changes my daily activities little. That is one of the curses of spending too much time in institutions of theological education; we immediately think of the seven (or seven hundred) different ways to understand the significance of the cross, and the whole thing becomes academic.

On other days—and more and more as I contemplate the practical needs of the church—it strikes me as the deeply wounding and healing path that we must travel if we are to witness to the gospel in a culture that has a distorted sense of its own goodness and its own entitlement, while having an increasing sense of its own loss of direction.

The Shape of a Life Renewed: From Individual Entitlement to Cruciform Community

It hardly seems necessary to demonstrate or argue for the fact that we live in a culture with a strong sense of entitlement. It's a normal part of childhood education to learn that individuals have a right to self-determination free from the interference of others. The presumption of natural human goodness coupled with a desire for this-worldly fulfillment has dramatically ramped up the expectations of modern Western individuals. Yet these expectations are rarely if ever met by an equal level of fulfillment, as manifested in the huge number of life-altering midlife crises that make it clear we haven't received the fulfillment to which we feel entitled, causing us then to shuffle the course of life in an effort to find this-worldly satisfaction before it's too late.

Individual rights, freedoms, and entitlements constitute the basic vocabulary of the secular political sphere as well. In high school I had a clarifying experience when I realized that the primary purpose of our civil government is to ensure we have the space—the freedom—to pursue these matters of individual entitlement: bodily safety, upward mobility, material comfort, the freedom to determine our own moral norms, a two-car garage, that is, the free pursuit of an often-shifting "happiness." While this may well be a decent basis on which to govern civil society, it makes the cultivation of Christian spirituality a profoundly countercultural experience.

Make no mistake: this isn't a conservative tirade against government benefits distributed to particular groups or individuals. Whatever the merits or lack thereof of such programs, conservative criticism of them simply reinforces the same individualistic sense of entitlement so widespread in our culture.

Consider, for instance, this recent piece in the *Yale Daily News* regarding proposed changes in Social Security that would allow for individual investment accounts:

> Conservatives are promising to fundamentally change the American political landscape by transforming those with little stake in society into the motivated owners of Wall Street stocks, health insurance accounts and homes. As it turns the blue-collar wage earner into an investor, the Bush administration's proposal for Social Security reform—centered on the voluntary investment of 4 percent of an individual's taxable income in cautious bonds and stock funds—is the beginning of this revolution. It's also what Democrats fear most: new legions of Republican voters marching to the tune of individualism, choice and ownership—not entitlement.[3]

Despite any potential significance of this policy shift, it is not revolutionary at all. It is merely reinforcing what everyone thinks his or her rights are: to unlimited happiness and choice. Conservatives are simply saying that they can better deliver that to which individuals sense they are entitled. When political debates rage over a distinction between "individualism" and "entitlement," Christians ought to realize that the ethos of the culture in which we find ourselves is one that is essentially at odds with the cruciform way of life to which we are called.

Yet mainline Protestants have struggled to witness faithfully to the gospel in the midst of such a culture of entitlement. We have not always been good exegetes of the culture. At times our conflation of American social and political ideals with the foundational principles of the Christian life has been unselfconscious, unintentional. One book on the history of the "cure of souls" has a subtitle that tells the story well: *A History of Pastoral Care in America: From Salvation to Self-Realization.*[4]

For the Protestant liberal tradition, this accommodation to contemporary American culture became programmatic and self-conscious, grounded in a belief in the inevitable progress of culture and the notion that this cultural progress is the primary means through which God reveals his will for the church.[5]

If evangelicals have been less self-conscious about their appropriation of the prevailing cultural ethos, they have been no lesser offenders. Consider the following observation about Christian bookstores, establishments that are by and large patronized by evangelicals: "The nation's Christian bookstores are full of self-help works addressing all the classic issues of our therapeutic culture— from failed relationships and low self-esteem to addiction and obesity—mixing the jargon of the self-actualization . . . movements with scriptural passages and the language of the pulpit."[6]

Self-help programs seeking the advancement of individuals by giving formulas through which their own hard work will bring betterment and satisfaction in this life are not going to cut it if we are hoping to address the deep and eternally significant spiritual needs of a culture beginning to sense its own loss of direction. I have yet to meet the person whose life was transformed by a self-help work who has not, soon thereafter, sought yet another temporary transformation through the next revolutionary formula on the market.

When we begin by assuming our own inherent goodness, seeking only the space or the right formula to allow our goodness to assert itself and yield the satisfaction we crave, we end up a frustrated and unsatisfied culture seeking therapy to work out an unwelcome sense of shame (though we call it by other names).

The point of this brief discussion is not to ridicule the culture or the church or any parties within it. The point is that *we are suffering from being deeply embedded in a post-Christian culture without a clear memory of the human condition and without a vision for the distinctive way of life to which we are called.* To put it mildly, we have a profound need for freedom from the guilt of sin and for a vision of life renewed by the power of the Holy Spirit; for the forgiveness of the cross and the cruciform way of life.

The Reformed tradition can help us here. In contrast to an emphasis on individual entitlement rooted in a notion of inherent human goodness, a Reformed understanding of the Christian life takes seriously the effects of sin and looks to the cross of Christ as the pattern for the Christian life. When Calvin says "the sum of the Christian life is self-denial," he is summarizing a way of life that, if we were to embrace it, would make us a remarkably *alternative* community, a royal priesthood for a culture in confusion (1 Peter 2:9).

Catching a glimpse of this life requires us to be open to paradox, one about which Jesus was clear with his call to the disciples: "If any want to become my followers, let them deny themselves and take up their cross and follow me. For those who want to save their life will lose it, and those who lose their life for my sake will find it" (Matthew 16:24–25). The path of fulfillment, of truly finding ourselves—the path that leads to resurrection unto life—is the path of self-denial.

There are several key dimensions to a Reformed vision for life as a perpetual cross, lived in conformity to Christ. I have space here to mention only three, but they will be sufficient for our purpose. A Reformed vision for the Christian life of self-denial is eschatalogical, earthy, and communal in orientation.

1. Self-denial is *eschatologically oriented* (to the end of time), because we live awaiting the consummation of the kingdom, and until then we "groan inwardly while we wait for adoption, the redemption of our bodies" (Romans 8:23). Christ has broken the power of sin once for all, but this will not be fully manifest in us until Christ returns. Until that time, the Christian life is marked by a struggle to realize progressively within ourselves what Jesus has already accomplished for us (the defeat of sin).

In this age we daily walk the path of the cross, putting to death the sin in us by the power of the Holy Spirit, living to righteousness, and looking forward to the day when the struggle will be over. Reformed theologians have called this the "mortification of the flesh" and the "vivification of the Spirit." Given that we live between the time of Christ's definitive defeat of sin and the ultimate manifestation of Christ's victory, Calvin called the church to "meditate on the future life," gaining confidence by looking forward to the ultimate experience of that true fulfillment in Christ that awaits us. Free from the illusion that our greatest dreams will be met in this life, we can loosen our grip on the things of this world, cease the search for ultimate satisfaction here and now, and deny ourselves the lusts of the flesh.

2. This life of self-denial is also *earthy*, and by this I mean that it stands in contrast to a mere otherworldly spiritual inwardness. Christian self-denial is not a retreat into a somber inward piety, but zeal, within and over against the culture of entitlement, to proclaim Christ with our lives. As Karl Barth said:

Self-denial in the context of following Jesus involves a step into the open, into the freedom of a definite decision and act, in which . . . that man takes leave of himself, of the man of yesterday, of the man he himself was . . . because what matters is not now himself but that he should do at all costs that which is proposed and demanded, having no option but to decide and act in accordance with it—cost what it may. "For God's sake do something brave," was once the cry of Ulrich Zwingli. . . . Not feel, or think, or consider, or meditate! Not turn it over in your heart and mind! But do something brave. If it is to this that Jesus calls man in his discipleship, there can be no avoiding genuine self-denial.[7]

3. This radical step into "the freedom of a definitive decision" is also profoundly communal, always outwardly focused, toward God and our neighbor. Such a life together would be a profound witness to a culture turned inward toward the self. Our guide for this is the story of Jesus, which we are called to make the pattern of our own lives. Christ's denial of himself to the point of death on the cross was *obedience to the Father* (Luke 22:42) and was for *our sake* (John 15:13). Indeed, Jesus repeatedly exhorted his followers to *assist him* in resisting the temptation to choose his own will over his Father's (Matthew 26:38–46).

The ideal held up in the New Testament is a *community* whose life is marked by obedience that often requires bearing the cross, denying ourselves, within and for the sake of that community of believers. Through a life characterized by self-denial we complete "what is lacking in Christ's afflictions for the sake of his body, that is, the church" (Colossians 1:24).

The Reformed vision for the Christian life calls us to live as a cruciform community, serving one another and witnessing to the gospel in an individualistic culture of entitlement, while we look forward to the consummation of the kingdom. As Calvin says, the Lord "teaches us to travel as pilgrims in this world," which frees us up for radical obedience and self-denial, knowing that our true home awaits us and we can engage this world in self-denial without counting the cost.[8]

Cruciform Community, Scripture, and Homosexuality

Cultivating a community life of self-denial will in itself be a step in a biblically, Christ-centered, and Reformed direction. But I'm convinced that it also relates directly to numerous deep struggles in the church. Our struggle with materialism is not an issue prominent in our denominational consciousness, though it ought to be, and it certainly relates directly to life as cruciform community. The call to self-denial is just beneath the surface of those matters about which there *is* much national controversy, such as the authority and interpretation of Scripture, the nature of church unity, matters of life (abortion and euthanasia), our social witness in global politics, and sexual ethics.

I have chosen to deal briefly with the matter of Scripture and somewhat more substantively with the issue of homosexual practice, simply because this is the most divisive issue at present, being thrust from the margins into the center of ecclesial debate by a very vocal minority in the church.

The question I put to myself is this one: How does the call to live as a cruciform community, looking forward to Christ's return, and engaging the world with a passion for the gospel, relate to how we read Scripture in general and address homosexual practice in particular? I do not pretend to offer any "Definitive Guidance." Rather, the following is my initial attempt to think through these issues in terms of our calling to live as a cruciform community.

It's no secret that just underneath our current moral debates in the church, including the debate over homosexual practice, is a foundational struggle over the authority and proper methods of interpreting Holy Scripture. As a cruciform community, when we approach the Holy Scriptures as readers and hearers of the Word of God, we must have a deeply humble posture, believing God will reveal to us his will, guide us in our faith and life together, exposing our lusts and our misdirected agendas, and showing us the path of love and obedience. Any hermeneutic (method of interpretation) that would preclude this approach to the text—that would place us over the text of Scripture—is a hermeneutic driven by self-assertion rather than self-denial.

What is so troubling today is that, in so many quarters of our church, the Bible is prohibited from saying anything we don't want to hear. When we read the Bible this way, we offer the world nothing better than the stereotypical religiosity with which Marx and Feuerbach had a field day (that is, religion is, at best, a projection of what we like about ourselves, or, at worst, a means by which a group violently asserts itself over the marginalized). Interpreting Scripture is hard work and sometimes, even after all the best efforts of gifted exegetes (interpreters) have been put forth, we are still surrounded by complexity and ambiguity. Yet the complexities and ambiguities that surround the hermeneutical enterprise ought not to be an excuse for saying there is no possibility of offering a reading of the text that is convicting and calls for transformation.[9]

Invoking complexities and degrees of ambiguity as a means of avoiding the *sensus literalis* (plain meaning) of a text is the result of a deep unease over how the message of the text might otherwise redirect our lives.

The Westminster Larger Catechism asks, "How is the Word of God to be read?" The catechism provides this answer:

> The Holy Scriptures are to be read with an high and reverent esteem of them; with a firm persuasion that they are the very Word of God, and that he only can enable us to understand them; with desire to know, believe, and obey the will of God revealed in them; with diligence, and attention to the matter and scope of them; with meditation, application, self-denial, and prayer.[10]

Approaching the Scriptures with such a posture, our minds can be opened to the Spirit's transformative work through the Word, rather than being conformed to and enslaved by the spirit of the age. Reading the biblical texts as the church is a spiritual exercise that requires us to have answered the radical call to discipleship in the affirmative. In other words, our hermeneutic must be a function of that commitment to the *imitatio Christi* (the imitation of Christ).

The debate over homosexual practice in the church is a good paradigmatic case that illustrates the subject of this chapter, that is, our call to live out the gospel with its implications for a life of self-denial in community. The struggle over the propriety of homosexual practice in the mainline church really is less about discerning what the Scriptures teach and more about figuring out what we are going to do with that teaching. As world-renowned New Testament scholar and Anglican bishop N. T. Wright has said of Paul's categorical prohibition of homosexual practice in Romans 1:26–27: "[I]t is clear that he regards homosexual practice as a dangerous distortion of God's intention. It is quite logical to say that we disagree with Paul . . . . What we cannot do is to sideline this passage as irrelevant to Christian ethical discourse . . . or to pretend that it means something other than what it says."[11]

Having sifted through the most compelling arguments for a nontraditional reading of the relevant biblical texts and the whole trajectory of God's design for human sexuality as presented in Scripture, I am convinced we are left with a couple of options: we can sideline those passages and the whole trajectory of God's design as "irrelevant to Christian ethical discourse," or we can be willing to hear the hard word and seek to discern what it means for our life together. So, how do we respond to the biblical prohibition of homosexual practice?

I suspect that the significant minority in the church (about 30 percent)[12] who are willing to set aside or to modify the Bible's teaching on homosexual practice are struggling, probably below the conscious level, with an understandably guilty conscience—a struggle with which *all* of us ought to resonate. That is, absent a consistently cruciform way of life throughout the Presbyterian Church (U.S.A.), it seems cruel that we would ask one group to live in radical self-denial—celibacy if sexual reorientation and marriage do not seem feasible.[13]

How can we ask this of homosexuals when we do not understand *ourselves*—the whole church—to have been called to such radical self-denial as a whole approach to life before Christ's return? How can we ask this of homosexuals when we are consistently lax on other matters of biblical sexual ethics, such as abstaining from premarital sex and living in fidelity in marriage? Incidentally, evangelicals cannot claim the higher moral ground here, as the rate

of divorce among evangelicals is at least equal to that of the surrounding entitlement culture.[14]

Charges of hypocrisy are therefore often laid at the feet of those who seek
to heed the biblical prohibition of homosexual practice, those who call "*this*
group of sinners" to repentance, and this charge is totally understandable.

When we put the clarity of the Scriptures on homosexuality next to our current unfaithfulness in other related ethical areas, not to mention our general
capitulation to the culture of entitlement, I believe we can take one of two
paths: We can call for a consistently cruciform life, including on matters of
sexual ethics (among both heterosexuals and homosexuals); or we can bring
nearer to completion our accommodation to a culture of entitlement, embrac-
ing a path of supposed personal fulfillment, whether that leads us to premarital sex, divorce without biblical warrant, or homosexual practice. In all
seriousness, either approach would have the virtue of being consistent.

It should be clear from what I have said thus far that I do not think taking
the latter route, setting aside the biblical prohibition of homosexual practice,
would be an all-of-a-sudden departure into an ascendant liberalism. On the
contrary, it may be better to think of it as a definitive sign that we have fallen
into a deep slumber, riding on a train with an engineer whose main concern
is to keep moving in the same direction, in the hopes that we will not be star-
tled by any emergency braking or an alert discussion about whether or not we
are in fact headed down the right track.

The call of the New Testament gospel is a call to a consistently cruciform
community! To respond to this call, to hope in the coming of the kingdom,
and to "do something brave" amidst a culture of entitlement—this is the path
of the church whose life is conformed to Jesus Christ.

With an eschatological orientation, we all need to recognize that the crav-
ing we have—the longing for fulfillment—is not one that will be satisfied until
Christ returns and restores all things. The "redemption of our bodies" that we
will then experience will set us free from the struggle; in the days between
now and then, as we await the Lord, we are sustained by his Spirit, who enables
us to live in joyful cruciform community.

New Testament scholar Richard Hays has noted that those "who demand
fulfillment now, as though it were a right or a guarantee, are living in a state of
adolescent illusion."[15] And he continues by commenting on the relationship
between homosexuals and single heterosexuals, noting that a homosexual is

in precisely the same situation as the heterosexual who would like to marry
but cannot find an appropriate partner (and there are many such); sum-
moned to difficult, costly obedience, while "groaning" for the "redemption

of our bodies" (Romans 8:23). Anyone who does not recognize this as a description of authentic Christian existence has never struggled seriously with the imperatives of the Gospel, which challenge and frustrate our "natural" impulses in countless ways.[16]

The decidedly communal nature of the cruciform life calls *the whole community to feel obligated to nurture, love, and support those struggling to live faithfully in the single life.* Especially for the sake of welcoming homosexuals, but also for the sake of ministering to those heterosexuals whom God has called to the single life, we need to stop treating singles in the church as though they are naturally waiting for something more in this life. ("Singles" groups in the church usually become contexts whose aim is to get people out of singleness!) We Protestants especially need to reconsider our understanding of the single life and to recognize that some people are called to be single and celibate for the sake of the kingdom. When we close the door to the single life as a vocation that people can live out imaginatively, we effectively constrain homosexuals to an isolated existence on the margins of the community.

Let me be blunt: no community has the right to reiterate the biblical call for homosexuals to live lives of celibacy if that community is not willing to answer the biblical call to love, to support, to nurture, and to groan with them as we all long for the redemption of our bodies. *We are called to a consistently cruciform way of life.*

As we aim for consistency, I'm convinced that the most pressing issue for the church in matters of sexual ethics is how we understand and help one another to live in marriage, if God has called us to this lifelong commitment to love another person.

There are a great many aspects of marriage that we need to wrestle through, self-consciously aware of the impact of the surrounding culture of entitlement. Not the least of these aspects is the management of expectations; we need to keep this eschatological orientation. Married persons, too, inwardly groan for the redemption of their bodies. There is something about traditional marriage vows that captures this key point: when we say, "For better, for worse," we are actually *promising to love this person even if the marriage makes things "worse" for me.* Behind that traditional vow is a profound recognition of the fallenness of creation and all our relationships, and a call to genuine *love* that is willing to endure radical self-denial.[17] In other words, it strikes me as a deeply cruciform promise, for the cross was the ultimate expression of Jesus' self-denial for the sake of us, whom he loves (Ephesians 5:25). Such love creates an inviolable bond.

These are, of course, only the beginnings of a conversation we need to be having in the church for years in the future. It will take decades to reshape the ethos of the church such that our assumptions about life before Christ returns have more to do with patiently bearing the cross than they do with finding satisfaction in the freedom for self-determination.

One of the remarkable things about postmodern culture is the fact that many people—especially young people—no longer believe in the entitlement-satisfaction myth. And they are looking for communities wherein they can live out a different vision for life.

If they are not drawn to Presbyterian churches, it won't be because we have asked too much of them, but because *we haven't asked enough.* May we begin being alternative communities, by witnessing to Jesus Christ through cross-bearing congregations, communities whose love for one another and obedience to Jesus Christ offer a foretaste of the kingdom.

Questions for Discussion

1. What do you think that the PC(USA) most needs today? Your congregation?
2. Do you agree that American culture is totally or mostly at odds with the Christian way of life set forth in Scripture?
3. Do you agree with the author's proposal for dealing with the issue of homosexuality in the life of the church? Why or why not?

Chapter 13

Who Needs the Church?

Barbara G. Wheeler

*B*ack in the 1960s, when I was part of the next generation, the path to rebellion was clearly marked. If you wanted to show your parents and the rest of the establishment that your goals and values were different from theirs, you knew where to go—to a commune, preferably in the Haight-Ashbury section of San Francisco—and what to do—tune into hip music; turn on to illegal substances and love, which was allegedly free; drop out of the rat race for money, success, and middle-class respectability; and maybe even get arrested in a demonstration for civil rights or against the Vietnam War.

Most of us did not do any of those things, but the very existence of a counterculture helped all of us, even timid kids like me, to imagine something different from the world of consumerism, cold war, and racial segregation into which we had been born.

Church Membership as a Countercultural Stance

Where is the counterculture today? Where can you go, what can you do, to rebel against the establishment, to demonstrate that you do not share the ideas, goals, and values that most people hold in contemporary America?

My answer to this question may surprise you. I don't think you'll find today's counterculture among the young. Despite superficial differences in dress, music, and comfort with technology, contemporary kids and their parents have remarkably similar values. Where you can go to rebel these days is to a church, perhaps especially one that has ties to the Reformed, Presbyterian tradition. What you can do—if you really want to be different from many of your friends and perhaps much of your family as well—is become a member.

This article originally appeared under the same title as a booklet in the Price H. Gwynn Church Leadership Series (Louisville, KY: Geneva Press, 2004).

This concept is probably not news to you. Within our lifetimes, we have crossed a major cultural divide, in this country and other Western societies. Although levels of participation in the institutions of organized religion have varied a lot in American history and have usually been lower than people think, until very recently most people felt obliged to explain why they did not hold traditional beliefs and belong to established congregations. Now the pressure is to explain not why one doesn't believe and belong, but why one *does*. One of my hobbies, as I travel around the country, is to read the personal ads in local papers. More and more, among the undesirable characteristics, in a person being sought, is organized religion—it's not as bad as smoking, but in some parts of the country, it's close.

The ads reflect a general cultural mood. It is fine to be spiritual, to pray, to read sacred scriptures, and to believe in supernatural realities such as ghosts, guardian angels, astrological forces, even God. But religious institutions are widely viewed today as unnecessary or worse. People accuse them of very serious offenses, such as wastefulness—the older, well-established ones especially, say the critics, use scarce charitable dollars for their own maintenance rather than other people's needs.

Another charge is hypocrisy. Some congregations are bitterly conflicted even while they preach forgiveness and love. They tend to narrowness, ignoring what is good in other religious traditions as well as what is faulty in their own, and almost all are discriminatory in one way or another. Social commentators often say that 11 a.m. on Sunday is the most segregated hour of the week, and, indeed, most congregations do exclude people, either by moral criteria or by making certain racial, cultural, or economic groups feel unwelcome. In the face of such sharp criticisms, choosing to join the kinds of religious groups to which most of you belong is indeed a countercultural act.

Choosing a Presbyterian church is more unusual still. Presbyterians, says a historian friend of mine, have been losing market share in America from their earliest decades here. The Calvinist ideas on which our tradition rests—the sovereignty of God, the helplessness of humanity, the pervasiveness of human sin—have never had mass appeal to optimistic, self-reliant Americans. Presbyterians' preference for plainness of style and our emphasis on words and reason rather than pictures and feelings have helped to prevent our kind of Protestantism from becoming a popular movement in American culture, where expression and emotion count for a lot. If you are a member of a Presbyterian church, you are an unusual sort of American indeed.

Recent Religious Trends

Recent religious trends in America have been much studied and well publicized. Most people in this society (over 90 percent) believe in God and say they lead spiritual lives, but the majority does not participate regularly in a congregation. Those who do join one are not likely to be interested in the organized, denominational side of religious life, or in longstanding religious traditions, especially the Calvinist stream that has come to be called "Reformed." When Americans' location or life circumstances or interests change, they may well change their religious identity too. We have become a nation of religious switchers. Finally, whatever Americans believe and belong to, they tend to regard as a private choice, something one keeps to oneself, rather than a public act—a view that is very much at odds with the Presbyterian conviction that God is at work in the whole world, not just the religious portion of it.

So who has made the wiser choice? The majority, who are free to graze for spiritual nourishment among all the great religions, who don't have to put up with bureaucracy and old-fashioned ideas, who get to protect their privacy? Or you who have chosen the less popular way, casting your lot with one Presbyterian church that links you to an organized denomination, to an older tradition, and to life out in the world?

If you've done the latter, you have, I think, made the better choice. In fact, I believe that, in the long run, you have no choice. For people of Christian faith, the only viable option is life together, over time, in a community that has come into being for the purpose of praising and serving God in concert with all God's other people, in all places and in all times.

The claim I have just made—that you can't be a person of Christian faith without the church—is pretty extreme. To back it up, I need to take a moment to define what I mean by faith, Christian faith in particular. Faith, as I am using the word, is not doctrines or specific teachings about God, Jesus Christ, salvation, sin, and the rest. Doctrines are important. The best of them tell us who God is, and if we care about God, we want to know that. But doctrines are complex, and you have to sort out the good from the bad. Faith is profound but very straightforward. Faith is simply the acknowledgment that God is God, and we are not God. God has come very close to us, even sent God's son, we Christians believe, to live as one of us. You cannot get more intimate than that. We are also made in God's image. We can look into the face of another human being and see the face of Christ, but still we are not God. Ultimately, says a famous old Reformed catechism, we are not our own; we belong to God, who is much more and much better than we are.

From what I can tell, many of today's spiritual seekers do not share my conviction that we belong to a God beyond ourselves. They seem to expect to find the spirit they are seeking inside, "a spark of the divine in every person," some of them like to say. On their terms, believing on your own, by yourself, makes sense, because (as they see it) what is needed to give life richness and depth is within you, a seed that needs only to be watered and fed.

But I do not think that that is true. The God who has made my life different from what it would have been in the ordinary course of things has powers I do not, which is fortunate, because even at my best I am not very good. I am not strong enough to resist temptations, including the greatest of them, which is to use good things for evil purposes. I cannot save myself, and even when God reaches out to me, I still can resist and lose God. To keep me, and all of us, from doing that—to ensure that we can persevere in the faith and not lose God—God has given us the church.

At first glance, churches hardly seem to be up to the challenge of helping us to stay aligned with God. Churches are often no better at that than other institutions, and sometimes they are worse. They can be self-serving, self-righteous, politicized, judgmental, dishonest.

Skeptical outsiders are not the only ones who point these things out. By the end of the church's first few decades, Saint Paul, who established many of the early congregations, could already see how bad church life could get: Not even the pagans, he wrote, do some of the things he witnessed in churches (1 Corinthians 5:1). John Calvin, who founded our Presbyterian wing of the church, insisted that no church anywhere has had or ever will have an unblemished record (*Institutes of the Christian Religion* 4.1.14 [1559]). What the nonjoiners say is true: churches are human institutions, and they are riddled with human failings.

And yet churches are also God's way of providing what people of faith need and cannot get anywhere else. In *The Muppet Movie*, Ralph the Dog sings a sad ballad about women to Kermit, who is drowning his sorrows in a bar after running afoul of Miss Piggy: "You can't live with 'em," Ralph croons, but "You can't live without 'em." Churches too.

How Churches Preserve Faith

I want to list for you three ways, in ascending order of importance, that, for all their defects and faults, churches are indispensable for people of faith who have found a God beyond themselves whom they do not want to lose.

First, *the church makes it possible for us to believe in God without doing too much harm.* The spirituality folks will tell you that religion is cool, joyful, and fulfilling, but they fail to mention the downside. Religion also does terrible damage—it demeans, hurts, even kills. Every form of national, ethnic, racial, class, and sexual prejudice has had religious backing at one time or another; every war ever fought has been blessed by religious leaders somewhere. "They preached a gospel of love," said a historian about Christians throughout the last millennium, "but they served a God of vengeance." Religion has been used to humiliate and oppress not only on battlefields but also in churches, homes, and schools. As I said earlier, we human beings are experts at using God's finest gifts to us, like faith in God, to advantage ourselves, diminish others, and defy God.

How do churches help us to have faith without corrupting it? Well, not all do, and none does all the time. Whole churches as well as individual leaders have committed the crimes and offenses I just listed. All of us who belong to churches should apologize for their offenses, perhaps even make reparations for them. But some churches also build in safeguards against their own misdeeds. While firmly believing the truth that they teach, they also regularly remind themselves that no single church or religious tradition has the only truth or the whole truth, and that God loves and works in the world just as much as God loves and helps the church. Humility and self-correction can become a regular pattern and practice of church life.

Other protections are built into the very fact of being a believing community that exists for any length of time in a particular place. People form opinions about that church, and they can be asked for feedback about which of our ideas and actions strike them as godly and which seem to be the opposite. If we really listen to what they say and change our ways when we are misusing our faith, we can have the joys and comforts of faith in God, just like the people who keep their spirituality to themselves. We also can have some protection that the spiritual individualists do not. We are protected by others against doing wrong in God's name, and losing touch with God in the bargain.

Second, *the church keeps us bound to each other*. Really? you may be thinking. Have you ever witnessed a church fight? Lots of people who do not join churches stay away because they have seen how vicious Christians can be to each other—and not just to other brands of Christians, but also to the members of their own denominations and even congregations. Almost every other kind of organization, say the refugees from church conflicts, is warmer and more welcoming than the church.

That is often true, but God also hates walls and divisions and intends to save the world by breaking them down. If we want to stay close to God, we need to participate in this barrier-breaking project, not frustrate it. Churches, for all their terrible mistakes, have a unique power to do that, because God established churches to call into God's service everyone God cares enough about to die for, which is everyone.

The community of God has no barriers to membership, not even sin. Christ died for us *while* we were sinners, didn't wait until we got over it. No club, no association, no nation, no multinational agency can say the same. When the church lives up to its charter, nothing divides its members. No one, no human being operating alone—even the most open, tolerant, and accepting—has the power to be as radically accepting as God when God established God's covenant with the church. People who wouldn't come together for any other reason, who don't share nationality, race, or opinions, who don't even like each other, can draw close to each other here, because God chose all of them. Because God's goal for the world is to put us all on the same footing, when we come close to each other, we come and stay close to God.

Last, *the church keeps us from losing God by keeping the faith.* The church's reputation, however, is otherwise. The most common suspicion about organized, established churches is that they are spiritually dead—empty shells of bureaucracy and tradition where God used to hang out but no longer does. Budgets, staff, politics, programs, and all those other members are distractions, people think. It is much easier to have a vibrant faith and to stay close to God in an exclusive one-on-one relationship, just me and God loving each other in private, with no institutional interruptions.

And that is correct—*sometimes.* As in any other romance, when things are going well, just the two of you is plenty. When the cares and troubles of life bear down, however, two is rarely enough, especially if the one you love is hurting you or failing to prevent you from being hurt. Then you need other people. None of us is strong enough to continue loving God in the bad times, when it feels as if God does not care about our pain and may even be causing it. Such moments happen to all of us. Every believer at some time has felt abandoned and punished by God.

Whoever wrote the psalms, the most joyful and magnificent songs in praise of God ever composed, wrote this and many passages like it:

> You have put me in the depths of the Pit,
>   in the regions dark and deep. . . .
> I, O LORD, cry out to you. . . .
>   I suffer your terrors; I am desperate.
> Why do you cast me off?
> Why do you hide your face from me?
>   Psalm 88:6, 13a, 15b, 14

In moments like these—when God is far away, not honeymooning with us, and when our faith is weak or nonexistent—we need the church, all those other lovers of God who, in the tough times, keep the faith for us.

An Example of the Church Being the Church

As I was writing, a friend called and told me a remarkable story. She had gone to church that day, in the small New England city where she lives. The minister opened the service by expressing his horror at an incident that had made newspaper headlines that week, the brutal assault of a women in the city's park. Then he announced that the victim, who had survived both rape and being dragged across a highway, was a deacon in that church, and in fact had been mailing cards to homebound church members when the crime occurred. He named the woman, and she came forward and spoke. She said simply that as she had endured the attack, she felt that her fellow church members were with her, bearing her up, and she thanked them and thanked God for them.

At the most terrible moment of her life, when God must have seemed very far away, trust in God was possible because she knew that others, including those whose cards she had held in her hand, were believing, trusting, and loving God for her, until she was strong enough to do it again for herself, and for them.

Church nonattenders have a point: going to church may not help us to be more spiritual people in the good times. When everything is going right, we may be able to have more fun with God by ourselves. But the church does something more important: It keeps us close to God through the difficult days and nights, when spiritual pleasure is out of the question.

As many of you probably know, if you stick with a congregation for better and for worse, sharing your faith when God gives you a lot of it, you too will receive faith from others at the desperate moments when you can't find your own. At moments such as these the special strength of Reformed traditions may come to the forefront. Our religious outlook, which may seem sober and even severe when the world is bright and beautiful, helps us to find the assurance of God's faithful presence in times of sorrow and despair.

Congregations Are Essential for Faith

Congregations are essential. Over the long haul you cannot, I am pretty sure, remain a person of Christian faith without one. Sometimes you will also need, if you want to keep the faith, to call on the wider church.

One of the graduates of my seminary once told me the story of her first days in ministry. She was not yet unpacked when the daughter of a church member asked her to sit with them as the mother lay dying. The daughter came from another city, did not know any of the members of the congregation that our graduate had come to serve, so she could not summon them, even in spirit. But she called our graduate to be part of this life-changing event, not because she knew her, but because she was a Presbyterian minister. The minister represented the wider church that keeps the faith that had sustained the mother.

I asked our graduate what she thought was expected of her. "I think," she said, "that I was expected to bring God." Sometimes, when our congregation cannot be reached, we need the whole denomination and the church universal of which it is a part to bring us God, or to witness to the presence of God who is already with us.

And then the times come when no one, in our own church or any other on the current scene, seems to be close enough to God to bring God to us. No less a role model than Jesus found himself with this problem more than once— separated from God and low on faith, with no one to minister to him. His solution may come as a surprise to people who think they can have instant Jesus without the baggage of church tradition around him. Jesus turned to tradition. When he felt weak, alone, deserted by his friends and abandoned by God, he quoted traditional Jewish texts and teachings: "Do not put the Lord your God to the test"; "Let this cup pass from me"; "Father, into your hands I commend my spirit."

Again, Presbyterian tradition has special resources for such times. One of the cherished themes of Reformed tradition is respect for the witness of those who have preceded us in faith. This grounding in tradition, one of the features that makes Calvinism such a tough sell to cheerful, novelty-loving Americans, can help to meet our deepest needs when we are most alone.

Someone recently said that mainline churches are now really sideline churches. In one sense that is true, but this sideline is a healthy and productive one. As I have been saying, belonging to an established church is good for your soul. And churches like our Presbyterian ones are good for a world that desperately needs durable local communities, strong ties between local communities, wisdom from the past, and care for the earth and all God's creatures who live in it. You have made a good choice; in fact, a great one, one that I hope many, many more people will make in the years to come.

Questions for Discussion

1. Do you agree with the author's assertion that to be a church member today is "countercultural"? Why or why not?
2. How is organized religion regarded in your community? Positively? Negatively?
3. Discuss the author's view of the ways churches help Christians to sustain and to strengthen their faith. Do you agree or disagree?

Notes

ORIENTING PERSPECTIVES

ECCLESIA REFORMATA, SEMPER REFORMANDA: REFORMED AND ALWAYS TO BE REFORMED

Bibliography

Calvin, John. "The Necessity of Reforming the Church." Library of Christian Classics 22. *Calvin: Theological Treatises*, trans. J. K. S. Reid. Philadelphia: Westminster Press, 1954.

Dowey, Edward. "Always to be Reformed." In *Always Being Reformed: The Future of Church Education*, ed. John C. Purdy. Philadelphia: Geneva Press, 1985.

Gerrish, Brian. "Tradition in the Modern World: The Reformed Habit of Mind." In *Toward the Future of Reformed Theology*, ed. David Willis and Michael Welker. Grand Rapids: Eerdmans, 1999.

Ottati, Douglas. *Reforming Protestantism.* Louisville, KY: Westminster John Knox Press, 1995.

Nebelsick, Harold. *"Ecclesia Reformata Semper Reformanda." Reformed Liturgy and Music* 18, no. 2 (Spring 1984).

Steinmetz, David. "The Intellectual Appeal of the Reformation." *Theology Today*, Jan. 1, 2001, 459ff.

WHAT THE PRESBYTERIAN CHURCH (U.S.A.) NEEDS TODAY

CHAPTER 2: THE POWER OF PARADOX

1. Adapted from William P. Barker, *Teach Us to Pray* (Old Tappan, NJ: Fleming H. Revell, 1977).

CHAPTER 5: THE REFORMED THEOLOGICAL TRADITION: A WAY OF BEING CHRISTIAN

1. Brian A. Gerrish, *Saving and Secular Faith: An Invitation to Systematic Theology* (Minneapolis: Fortress, 1999), 56.

2. John M. Buchanan, *Being Church, Becoming Community* (Louisville, KY: Westminster John Knox Press, 1996), xii.

3. Dietrich Bonhoeffer, *Letters and Papers from Prison* (New York: Macmillan, 1953), 226.

4. Jürgen Moltmann, *The Passion for Life* (Philadelphia: Fortress Press, 1978), 22.

5. Paul Tillich, *The Shaking of the Foundations* (New York: Charles Scribner's Sons, 1948), 162.

CHAPTER 6: ACCORDING TO THE WORD OF GOD

1. Today's pluralists prefer to call themselves "Progressive Christians." But the theological liberalism that they profess represents a return to ancient paganism, an ideology that is neither progressive nor Christian. Thus "Regressive" is the label of choice in this essay.

2. *Princeton Theological Review* 20 (1922): 107–8.
Note: The author provides his own translations from the original languages for the passages cited.

CHAPTER 7: A RESOURCE FOR REGATHERING GOD'S PEOPLE

1. Henry G. Brinton, *Washington Post*, Oct. 19, 2003, B04.

2. Jack Rogers, "What Makes Us Distinctive as Presbyterians," video produced by the Covenant Network of Presbyterians, 2003.

3. *Book of Order* (Louisville, KY: Office of the General Assembly, 2002), G-14.0207.

4. Brian A. Gerrish, *Reformed Theology for the Third Christian Millennium* (Louisville, KY: Westminster John Knox Press, 2003), 6.

5. Ibid., 6.

6. Ibid., 7–8.

7. Letty Russell, *Church in the Round* (Louisville, KY: Westminster John Knox Press, 1993), 173.

CHAPTER 9: REFORMED AND EVER REFORMING: SIX THESES TOWARD THE REVISIONING OF THE CHURCH

1. For a helpful discussion of when and how these terms apply, see Final Report, Third World Conference on Faith and Order, August 15–28, 1952, Lund, Switzerland, *A Documentary History of the Faith and Order Movement, 1927–1963*, ed. Lukas Fischer (St. Louis: Bethany Press, 1963), esp. 96–100.

2. See Richard A. Horsley, *Bandits, Prophets, and Messiahs: Popular Movements in the Time of Jesus* (San Francisco: Harper San Francisco, 1988).

3. On this point, see Rowan Williams, *Resurrection: Interpreting the Easter Gospel* (London: Longman, Darton, & Todd, 1982; reprint, Cleveland, Ohio: Pilgrim Press, 2003).

4. See, e.g., Andrew F. Walls, *The Missionary Movement in Christian History* (New York: Orbis, 1996); Lamin O. Sanneh, *Whose Religion Is Christianity? The Gospel beyond the West* (Grand Rapids: Eerdmans, 2003); Lamin O. Sanneh, *Translating the Message: The Missionary Impact on Culture* (New York: Orbis, 1989); Luis N. Rivera, *A Violent Evangelism: Political and Religious Conquest of the Americas* (Louisville, KY: Westminster John Knox Press, 1992).

5. Darrell L. Guder, ed., *Missional Church: A Vision for the Sending of the Church in North America* (Grand Rapids: Eerdmans, 1998).

6. Catherine LaCugna, "The Practical Trinity," *Christian Century* 109 (July 15–22, 1992): 678–82.

7. See William Stacy Johnson, "Theology and the Church's Mission: Catholic, Orthodox, Evangelical, and Reformed," in *Reformed Theology: Identity and Ecumenicity*, ed. Wallace M. Alston Jr. and Michael Welker (Grand Rapids: Eerdmans, 2003), 65–81.

8. Many Americans seem content with the notion that the abuses of Abu Ghraib were an aberration. And yet it is now clear that mistreatment of prisoners and even torture found support at the highest levels of Washington. For substantiation of these claims, see *The Torture Papers: The Road to Abu Ghraib*, ed. Karen J. Greenberg and Joshua L. Dratel (Cambridge: Cambridge University Press, 2005); Mark Danner, *Torture and Truth: America, Abu Ghraib, and the War on Terror* (New York: New York Review of Books, 2005). For helpful analysis, see the following review: Noah Feldman, "Ugly Americans: The Laws of a War against Evil," *The New Republic* 232, issue 4,715 (May 30, 2005): 23–29.

9. For example, Maher Arar is a Syrian-born Canadian citizen who was detained on Sept. 26, 2002, by American authorities while he was changing flights with his wife and children in Kennedy Airport. Arar's infraction? He had a co-worker, who in turn had a brother—a person whom Arar says he barely knew—who was suspected of having links to Al Qaeda. Based on this slim thread of suspicion, and without being charged with any crime, Arar was chained and "renditioned" by the U.S. government to Jordan and then to Syria, where he was incarcerated for a year and subjected to acts of extreme physical torture. Though they made him confess under duress to many things, the Syrians concluded that Arar knew nothing of any value concerning terrorism. One of the most accessible accounts of this story is Jane Mayer, "Outsourcing Torture," *New Yorker*, Feb. 14, 2005, http://www.newyorker.com/fact/content/articles/050214fa_fact6, posted Feb. 2, 2005, accessed April 2005. See also www.maherarar.ca. What does the gospel say to this?

10. Interrogators have long known that the best way to extract information is not through brutality but through kindness. See Stephen Budiansky, "Truth Extraction: A Classic Text on Interrogating Enemy Captives Offers a Counterintuitive Lesson on the Best Way to Get Information," *The Atlantic* 295, no. 5 (June 2005): 32. Even the conservative *Weekly Standard* realizes this. See Reuel Marc Gerecht, "Against Rendition: Why the CIA Shouldn't Outsource Interrogations to Countries that Torture," *The Weekly Standard* 10, no. 3 (May 16, 2005): 21–26.

11. On Sept. 15, 2001, just days after the Sept. 11 attacks in New York, Pennsylvania, and Washington, D.C., a memorial service was held in the National Cathedral in Washington, D.C., which concluded with the choir and congregation singing "The Battle Hymn of the Republic." The conservative Presbyterian leader J. Gresham Machen once opposed this hymn as unchristian.

12. The classical just war perspective sets limits upon a war's commencement (i.e., authorization by a competent authority, a just cause, the goal of peace, use of force as a last resort, a reasonable chance of success, and a response that is in proportion to the aggression), its conduct (i.e., discriminating between combatants and noncombatants, and using only such force as is necessary), and its consequences (winners have responsibilities to losers). Preemptive war is justified only if attack is imminent, which it was not in Iraq. The concept of a "preventive war," waged to avert a hypothetical attack, has no support in the classical tradition.

13. America's leading expert on "just war," who himself has supported many recent wars, has argued that the war against Iraq was wrong. See Michael Walzer, *Arguing about War* (New Haven and London: Yale University Press, 2004), chap. 11.

14. Or when it is offered, it is singularly dismaying. We are told that because of the threat of terror we now have cause to "rethink the whole spirit of Just War arguments" (Chuck Colson, "Just War, Terror, and Pre-emption," Oct. 27, 2004, http://www.townhall.com/columnists/chuckcolson/cc20041027.shtml). In other words, our feeling of insecurity justifies us in attacking whenever and wherever we wish. Is that "evangelical"?

15. Douglas Jehl and David Johnston, "Rule Change Lets CIA Freely Send Subjects Abroad," *New York Times*, March 6, 2005, A1. Available online: http://query.nytimes.com/gst/abstract.html?res=F7061EFE35590C758CDDAA0894DD404482&incamp=archive:search.

16. That day the Web site "Presbyweb," which gives a daily reflection of what is being discussed in the secular and church presses, was replete with articles on the issues that drive the so-called "culture wars"—issues such as the growing power of religious "conservatives," disputes over gays (there were at least four that touched on this), "intelligent design" arguments, stem cell research, abstinence programs, and abortion. There was even a story about the abortion of sheep! I am thankful that there was one article about slavery in Niger. Yet even though there were three articles gleaned from the *New York Times*, there was nothing about the *Times* article on torture. And even though torture was discussed at a meeting of the PC(USA) Theological Task Force on Peace, Unity, and Purity of the Church on March 2–4, the two conservative commentators who were featured in Presbyweb that day chose to ignore the torture issue and not to write about it. See http://www.presbyweb.com/2005/Archive/0307.htm, accessed April 28, 2005. After I pointed out the omission, the story was run on Presbyweb on March 11, 2005.

17. For this particular way of framing my theology, I am indebted to a conversation many years ago with Jack Rogers.

18. This threefold form of the Word of God—i.e., revealed, written, and proclaimed—derives from Reformation teaching and has been revitalized in our day by Karl Barth, *Church Dogmatics*, I/1.

19. The literature from this movement includes Rick Warren, *The Purpose-Driven Church* (Nashville: Thomas Nelson Books, 1995), and Bill Hybels, *Becoming a Contagious Christian* (Grand Rapids: Zondervan, 1996).

20. Brian D. McLaren, *A Generous Orthodoxy: Why I Am a Missional, Evangelical, Post/Protestant, Liberal/Conservative, Mystical/Poetic, Biblical, Charismatic/Contemplative, Fundamentalist/Calvinist, Anabaptist/Anglican, Methodist, Catholic, Green, Incarnational, Depressed-yet-Hopeful, Emergent, Unfinished CHRISTIAN* (Grand Rapids: Zondervan, 2004); Doug Pagitt, *Reimagining Spiritual Formation: A Week in the Life of an Experimental Church* (Grand Rapids: Zondervan, 2004); Robert Webber, *The Younger Evangelicals: Facing the Challenges of the New World* (Grand Rapids: Baker, 2002); Robert Webber, *Ancient-Future Faith: Rethinking Evangelicalism for a Postmodern World* (Grand Rapids: Baker, 1999); Dan Kimball, *The Emerging Church* (Grand Rapids: Zondervan, 2003). See also the excellent article by Scott Bader-Saye, "The Emergent Matrix: A new kind of church?" *Christian Century* 121, no. 24 (Nov. 30, 2004): 20–27. I wish to thank Scott Collins-Jones, Brad Jackson, and members of the Central Jersey Cohort for their support in the thinking about what we mean by "church."

21. This point has been made by David Brooks, "A Natural Alliance: Coming Together to Fight Poverty," *New York Times*, May 26, 2003, A29.

CHAPTER 11: THE PRESBYTERIAN CHURCH OF 2050

1. Peter Gomes, *Sermons: Biblical Witness for Daily Living* (San Francisco: Harper San Francisco, 1998), 234.

CHAPTER 12: WHAT THE CHURCH NEEDS TODAY

1. John Calvin, *Institutes of the Christian Religion* (Philadelphia: Westminster Press, 1960), 3.8.1.

2. Ibid., 3.7.1.

3. Keith Urbahn, *Yale Daily News*, "Putting the Torch to a Culture of Entitlement," March 23, 2005.

4. E. Brooks Holifield, *A History of Pastoral Care in America: From Salvation to Self-Realization* (Nashville: Abingdon, 1983).

5. For a description of this complex movement and its changing shape over time, see William R. Hutchison, *The Modernist Impulse in American Protestantism* (Durham, NC: Duke University Press, 1992).

6. Paul Boyer, "Two Centuries of Christianity in America: An Overview," *Church History* 70, no. 3 (2001): 551.

7. Karl Barth, *Church Dogmatics*, trans. G.W. Bromiley (Edinburgh: T. & T. Clark, 1969), IV/2:539.

8. Calvin, *Institutes*, 3.7.3.

9. For a robust discussion of the complexities of postmodern hermeneutics that includes a defense of interpreting the biblical texts according to authorial intention, see Kevin J. Vanhoozer, *Is There a Meaning in This Text? The Bible, the Reader, and the Morality of Literary Knowledge* (Grand Rapids: Zondervan, 1998).

10. Westminster Larger Catechism Q. 157, in *Book of Confessions: Study Edition* (Louisville, KY: Westminster John Knox Press, 1999), 7.267.

11. N. T. Wright, *Romans*, in *The New Interpreter's Bible* (Nashville: Abingdon, 2002), 10:435. For a full exegetical treatment of the subject, see Robert Gagnon, *The Bible and Homosexual Practice* (Nashville: Abingdon, 2001). For more brief treatments of the two sides of the debate, see Robert Gagnon and Dan Via, *Homosexuality and the Bible* (Minneapolis: Fortress, 2003).

12. Presbyterian Panel, *Report: Ministries to Families and Same-Sex Issues*, The August 2000 Survey, 12.

13. The whole question of transformation of sexual orientation is one of those controversial issues that deals with both biblical theology and empirical evidence. Richard Hays is surely right when he makes this summary comment in his *The Moral Vision of the New Testament* (San Francisco: Harper, 1996), 393: "The cross marks the end of the old life under the power of sin (Romans 6:1–4). Therefore, no one in Christ is locked into the past or into a psychological or biological determinism."

14. See Ron Sider, *The Scandal of the Evangelical Conscience: Why Are Christians Living Like the Rest of the World?* (Grand Rapids: Baker, 2005), 18.

15. Hays, *Moral Vision*, 393.

16. Ibid., 402.

17. It must be said here that the self-denial we envision does not mean passive subjection in abusive relationships. Spousal abuse is most often committed by husbands, and the explicit biblical injunction regarding self-denial according to the pattern of the cross within the context of marriage applies to *them*: "Husbands, love your wives, just as Christ loved the church and gave himself up for her" (Ephesians 5:25). See David P. Gushee, "Suffering in Marriage (and Divorce)," chapter 7 of his *Getting Marriage Right: Realistic Counsel for Saving and Strengthening Relationships* (Grand Rapids: Baker, 2004).